GW00385444

Mark 'Chopper' Read is one of Australia's most controversial public figures. He is an ex-convict, author and celebrity. He is also a recording and performance artist.

One thing
led to
another

Mark 'Chopper' Read

One thing
led to
another

MACMILLAN
Pan Macmillan Australia

First published 2010 in Macmillan by Pan Macmillan Australia Pty Limited
1 Market Street, Sydney

Copyright © Mark Brandon Read 2010

The moral right of the author has been asserted.

All rights reserved. No part of this book may be reproduced or transmitted by any person or entity
(including Google, Amazon or similar organisations), in any form or by any means, electronic
or mechanical, including photocopying, recording, scanning or by any information storage and
retrieval system, without prior permission in writing from the publisher.

National Library of Australia
Cataloguing-in-Publication data:

Read, Mark Brandon, 1954–

One thing led to another / Mark Read.

ISBN: 9781405040464 (pbk.)

Read, Mark Brandon, 1954–
Criminals – Australia – Biography.

364.1092

Typeset in 12.5/16.5pt Sabon by Midland Typesetters Australia
Printed in Australia by McPherson's Printing Group

Papers used by Pan Macmillan Australia Pty Ltd are natural, recyclable products made from
wood grown in sustainable forests. The manufacturing processes conform to the environmental
regulations of the country of origin.

To Roy

CONTENTS

INTRODUCTION

I have written thirteen books, if you count the two adult fairytales I've published under my name. They've all been best-sellers. So, you might ask, why would Mark Brandon – or Chopper – Read write another one?

The answer is, my wife, Margaret, and my son Roy. Margaret Read, my friend of nearly thirty years, and wife of eight years, wants me to write a book that will help Roy get to know the real me; the real us.

The fact is, Margaret was never happy with the way the movie *Chopper* left things. As she says herself, later in this book, she wants to have something written that gives Roy a better understanding of who his parents are, especially his father.

When Andrew Denton interviewed me, a few years ago on *Enough Rope*, on ABC television, I suggested I might one day write the definitive book about a lot of things that have happened in my life. I also said that I write my books and allow the readers to make up their own minds about me and the stories I tell.

Well, I am not prepared to say this is the definitive book. That would be bragging. But, once again, and now with the help of Margaret and my mother, I am allowing the readers to make up their own minds.

One reader in particular, Roy Brandon Read.

Mark Brandon Read
October 2010

CHAPTER 1

THE FIRST DAY OF THE REST OF MY LIFE

If you're into clichés and, come on, who isn't, it was the first day of the rest of my life.

I've had a few of those over the years – like the day I went to Her Majesty's Prison Risdon in Tasmania, for what looked like being the rest of my natural life, to paraphrase Marcus Clarke in his novel about some other poor bugger, Rufus Dawes, stuck in Tasmania in the convict days. And it was for a murder Rufus didn't commit – I've had a few of those experiences, too.

However, this June 2001 first day of the rest of my life was different; this was the day that I was going home.

And no, not to Her Majesty's Prison Pentridge, the fine establishment that was my home for such a long time, but to another part of Melbourne for which I have a lot of affection – Collingwood. It's also home to a person for whom I have a lot, lot more than affection – Margaret Cassar, someone you're going to hear about a fair bit in this book. Some people, especially my mother, say she's the woman who has straightened me out, who has put my life back together. It's probably true. She's Maltese and if you think the Maltese Cross is some fancy emblem – well, you haven't seen an angry Margaret Cassar. That's a Maltese cross! In many ways, she is the term of my natural wife. Although we have been married for only eight years, we have known each other for much longer.

How I ended up making a phone call to her from chilly Hobart airport to let her know I was on my way back to Melbourne is like how I ended up anywhere – a long story. I won't cut it short. The journey to this particular phone call started when I shot Sidney Michael Collins.

I had been living in Launceston with Margaret. In 1991, when I had got out of Pentridge for the last time, after doing four and a half years following the shooting of Sammy the Turk, Margaret had agreed to move to Tasmania with me to be closer to my family. At that time, even though they were separated, my mother and father were living there, and my mother and sister still live there.

I had been cleared of the murder of Sammy the Turk, on the grounds of self-defence, but did time for arson and attempted murder. That's another long story, which we'll get to later.

For a long time while I was in Tasmania, I was keeping myself out of trouble, relatively speaking. We had a nice place at Newnham, a Launceston suburb. It backed up onto the Mowbray Golf Course and Ricky Ponting probably went past my house a few times when he was playing golf there, as he's a Mowbray boy. I might even have shot one of his golf balls. The ninth hole was right behind our house and I used to shoot the balls with my .22 calibre pump action rifle. I suppose the golfers wondered what had happened to them, but there were a lot of big black crows flying around and they probably thought they got 'em. I also made a pretty good living by gambling at the casino in Launceston. One day I won $50,000 playing roulette but, being Mark Read, I had to put it all back on the table. Yeah, Margaret, I know; I blew it all.

One of the reasons I liked Tasmania was that, at that time, it had the most lax gun laws in the country. I once had a reporter come and interview me about all my guns, and I gave a little display of my ability, shooting a bottle out of the hands of a local bloke by the name of Trent Anthony. It wasn't quite William Tell and the apple, but it was pretty fancy.

I am told you can still find it on YouTube. I am not real big on computers and the Internet, but someone has been keeping an eye on my appearances on my behalf. Apparently, there's a tonne of stuff about me. Type 'Mark Brandon Read' into Google and you get more than 1.5 million hits. Type 'Eric Bana' and you only get 1.4 million. Mark Chopper Read – still the original, still the best. Anyway, I'm digressing already. When you have had a rich life such as mine, there are just too many things to talk about.

While living in Tasmania, I'd also started hanging around with this Sidney Michael Collins, who was the leader of the Tasmanian branch of the Outlaws Motorcycle Club. One thing led to another and I had to shoot him.

We were in Evandale, a nice little village in Tasmania where they hold a penny farthing race every year. They have a lot of old-fashioned things in Tasmania. Evandale was where Collins was living at the time. He's not living there anymore. He's not even living – something else we will get to soon.

The day I shot him, we had been drinking at the Clarendon Arms in Evandale. It's a great little pub, which had a big open fireplace with a chair right next to it. After closing time, I'd sit a toy bear in the chair and shoot at it and other people would shoot at the bear too. So, we'd all be there in the Clarendon Arms after closing time, shooting at this poor bear that ended up with a lot of holes in him.

Anyway, after one of the times I'd been drinking in the Clarendon Arms, we went for a drive – Trent Anthony, Sidney Michael Collins and me. Collins was in the back of my car. Trent Anthony was driving and I was in the passenger seat. I turned around and shot Sidney Michael Collins.

The day before had been his birthday and I had given him a walking stick as a present. Now I thought to myself, 'The day after I gave him a walking stick for his birthday, I shot him in the guts.' He never saw the funny side of it.

When I shot him, he looked at me in pained disbelief and said, 'Why did you do that, Chopper?'

I said, 'You know why. You have been living out of my pocket ever since I've known you.'

He admitted that he had, having been borrowing money all the time and never paying it back.

I then asked him, 'Do you want one in the brain?'

'No,' he said, 'I won't give you up.'

A lot of people – especially me – have been questioned over a lot of things I've done or haven't done, inside and outside of jail, and a lot of these people have never given me up. Just like I have never given anyone up. I wouldn't have survived all those years in Pentridge with the likes of Russell 'Mad Dog' Cox if I were a dobber. When Sidney Michael Collins said he wouldn't give me up, I believed him that he wouldn't talk to the police.

So I said to Trent, 'Drive him to the hospital.'

That was a big mistake. Collins just wouldn't shut up. He kept talking to the police. And talking and talking.

I should have shot him in the head.

The incident became a huge story all over the place, with Chopper Read, the best-selling author, being charged with inflicting grievous bodily harm.

On 14 May 1992, I was charged in Launceston and, after a couple of trials that got more publicity than OJ Simpson's, I was eventually sentenced under the Dangerous Criminals Act. There were two trials because the first one ended in a hung jury. That seemed pretty strange to me. The jury had the evidence of Trent Anthony that I had shot Sidney Michael Collins. And, of course, they had the evidence of Collins, who was still talking.

When you shoot a bikie, there are, as often as not, a lot of people who want to shoot you back. The fact that I am alive today and writing this suggests that a lot of Sidney Michael Collins's bikie mates didn't take too kindly to him becoming a Crown witness. I can tell you, I certainly didn't. And I wasn't too pleased when Trent Anthony did too.

I had pleaded not guilty, of course, but there was still plenty of evidence against me – with even my books being used against me – but somehow we ended up with this hung jury and even more publicity. So, we had to go to another trial, at which I was found guilty. Being sentenced under the Dangerous Criminals Act – or whatever fancy name they had for this legislation in Tasmania – effectively meant I was never to be released because they thought I was a dangerous criminal who would offend again the moment I got out of prison. People always make a lot of assumptions about me. Can't think why!

When Sidney Michael Collins disappeared once and for all in 2002, while he was driving around in northern New South Wales, the police wanted to interview me. I always seem to get interviewed by the police when people disappear. I reckon that over the years I have been questioned about more than sixty murders. I have never been found guilty of any of them.

Anyway, in October these two coppers came to Melbourne from Casino, which is a town in northern New South Wales, not a gambling establishment. They wanted to question me, so I went along with my solicitor, Bernie Balmer, to the big police complex they've got on St Kilda Road. Ron Iddles from the Victorian homicide squad was there too. I told them all that I didn't know anything about Sidney Michael Collins's disappearance.

Apparently, he was travelling from the Gold Coast to somewhere in northern New South Wales to recover some money he reckoned he was owed. Nice to see he knew what it felt like to be owed money. Anyway, after his son had reported him missing, they found Collins's ute but they never found him.

The two New South Wales coppers wanted to know whether I had killed Sidney Michael Collins or might have been responsible for his disappearance. They seemed to have received a lot of information to the effect that I knew something about it. I had to put them straight. I told them I reckoned he had faked his own death and was probably living in a motel room some-where – this was all on the basis that I already knew him to be a shady individual.

I told the media at the time that the New South Wales police were harassing me and that the only reason they had come to Victoria was to go to the Spring Racing Carnival. I also told them I thought these coppers were putting bets on for Sid Collins at Flemington and Caul-field racetracks. Of course, the police denied the trip was timed to coincide with the racing carnival and claimed the detectives were following a routine line of inquiry. Routine lies of inquiry, more like it.

Whatever did happen to Sidney Michael Collins – well, who knows? The last I had heard of him, it was that he was hanging around with the Russian Mafia and helping to bring Russian brides into Australia. All I knew was that it was good riddance. He had caused me a lot of grief, and a lot of jail time.

Tasmania only has one real jail, Her Majesty's Prison Risdon, out in the boondocks behind Hobart. There's a prison farm at some place called Hayes but I never got to go there. The only farm that might have been a prison that I got to, as you will find out soon, was called Glen Air. Risdon Prison is sometimes called the Pink Palace because that's the colour they painted it when it was first built. Pink . . . for a jail? They're different in Tasmania, all right.

There have been a few well-known Risdon residents. There was Steve Randell, the Test cricket umpire, who got four years for touching up school kids. It seems that when the judge sentenced him to those four years, some of the girls who'd been his victims stood up at the back of the court and signalled four, like you do in cricket.

There was a bloke called Jeffrey Peter Radloff, who kidnapped a boy and left him in a suitcase under the wheels of a car in one of Hobart's main streets. Thankfully, someone found the suitcase before the kid got run over. In 2006, after doing his time for the kidnapping, Radloff was arrested and charged with trying to organise a breakout from Risdon.

There was also an accountant by the name of Colin Room, who ripped off half of Launceston.

And then there was Martin Bryant. He is the bloke who shot thirty-five people at Port Arthur on 28 April 1996. Thirty-five innocent people – that's the same number who died when the Westgate Bridge collapsed while it was being built. The Westgate bridge collapse was an awful accident. What Martin Bryant did was a slaughter of innocents.

One day, he was coming out of the infirmary and saw me through the fence. He walked up to me and, in that silly little voice of his, said, 'Hello, Mr Read.'

I looked him straight in the eye and said, 'Why did you do it?'

Again in that silly little voice, he said, 'I was eating my peas and suddenly the room was full of dead people.' He shot a lot of his victims in the Broad Arrow Café, in which people were eating their lunch.

Martin Bryant will never be released from Risdon; a fate I thought had also come my way.

I'll never forget the day Margaret came to Risdon to say goodbye to me. It was about a fortnight after I had been charged with the shooting of Sidney Michael Collins.

She was very tearful. I put my hand through the bars to touch her and the screws told me I couldn't. I never did warm to the screws in Tasmania. They were pretty ordinary. They wouldn't get a job in a place like Pentridge.

Anyway, Margaret and I didn't say a lot of words to each other. Our silences said everything. After I had got out of Pentridge, I had made a commitment to her to change my life, to stay out of prison. Six months later, here I was back in prison.

When Margaret did speak, she told me that she couldn't live like this anymore; that she was returning to Melbourne to put her life back together.

And I told her to go, that I realised she'd had enough of putting up with me.

'Go and pick up the pieces and get a new life,' I told her.

I was crying too.

We said our last goodbyes and Margaret headed off to make her way to Melbourne. She couldn't stay at our house in Launceston because the police had taken possession of it while looking for evidence.

They found plenty – my guns. I listed them all in one of my early books, *Chopper 2 – Hits and Memories*:

A Ruger ten-shot .22 carbine.

A Savage .22 bolt action rifle.

A Stirling .22 bolt action rifle.

A Sportco .22 bolt action rifle.

A .303 rifle.

An Ace .22.

A Baikal .22.

A Boito single barrel shotgun.

A sawn-off twelve-gauge shotgun.

There was also the small matter of there being more than enough (you can't have too much, can you?) ammo for all these guns, two rifle scopes, a set of nunchakus and a shoulder holster for a revolver.

With the house at Newnham out of bounds, Margaret was supposed to stay for a while with friends in Launceston, but they were frightened that some of Sidney Michael Collins's mates might make a call on her, so they asked her to move out. She went to stay at the Clarendon Arms Hotel, along with our dog, Nibbles, a Staffordshire cross. We've still got photos of Nibbles. He was a lovely dog. Michael Alexander, the publican at the Arms, said it was okay for Margaret and Nibbles to stay there.

A friend of mine by the name of Dave the Jew – more on him later too – came over to the Arms for a while, but the local police weren't too happy with that arrangement. Apparently, they thought Dave the Jew might interfere with some of their witnesses.

The police actually turned up at the Clarendon Arms, demanding to see Margaret, who was upstairs at the time.

Michael Alexander walked up to her and said, 'Margaret, don't come down now, there are twenty-two police waiting to see you.'

When she did come down, the police handed her an identikit photo of Dave the Jew, who, at the time, was standing right beside her. They asked Margaret if she recognised the person in the identikit photo. She said she had never seen him before in her life. Dave the Jew reckoned that was pretty quick thinking.

Whether it was or not, the police weren't making Margaret feel too welcome in Launceston, so she got on the boat at Devonport and sailed back to Melbourne that afternoon.

The funny thing is, the car, a big Ford Falcon, we were driving the day I shot Sidney Michael Collins was Margaret's. But at the end of the trials, the coppers gave it to Trent Anthony. Trent went off to Western Australia and I don't think I've heard of him, or the car, since.

After that day at Risdon when Margaret and I parted for what we both thought was the last time, I went to my prison cell and began thinking about my own life. I was wondering how I could put all the pieces back together. An attempted murder charge was hanging over my head. I thought that if I was found guilty and put in jail under the Dangerous Criminals Act, that was it, I would never see Margaret Cassar again. To get out, I needed the cards to fall in a way that seemed utterly impossible.

Thankfully, Michael Hodgman, QC and MP, heard about my case. He's a big shot in Tasmania. He once appeared on the front page of the *Hobart Mercury*, saying Australia should do away with the two-dollar note. The headline said, 'Look Who Is Big Noting Himself Again!' In Tassie, they kinda know what Michael is like, but like him anyway. And he was right about getting rid of the two-dollar note. It's gone.

Behind everything he does is a very clever lawyer. In fact, if he'd backed John Howard instead of that show pony Andrew Peacock in the Liberals leadership race, he might have become even more famous in Canberra and for more than being The Mouth from the South. He might have been the Federal Attorney-General. Anyway, after he fell foul of John Howard, he went back to Tasmania and got into state parliament, winning the seat of Denison, which is in Hobart. Michael's stint as a parliamentarian was one of the longest in Australian history.

They're a longstanding family of politicians, the Hodgmans. Michael's father was one, as was his brother

Peter. And his son Will is keeping the family tradition alive, as leader of the Liberal Party in Tasmania. In March this year, young Will nearly got to be the premier. That would have pleased Michael; his son being the premier at the same time that his favourite football team, Geelong, were the premiers.

Michael Hodgman QC MP thought the Dangerous Criminals Act was wrong, whether it was being applied to Mark Read or anyone else.

It was wrong, all right, because it was worse than the bloody Governor's Pleasure concept from the days of the old Tasmanian colony when the place was full of convicts. With the Dangerous Criminals Act, you didn't need just the Governor's Pleasure to get out, you needed the premier and the full state cabinet, and all on the same day.

And that was never going to happen.

If you know Hobart, you will know that Parliament House, where the premier and cabinet hang out, is down near Salamanca Place and that the governor lives in a big house up on the Domain, right out of town. And they're all busy people, certainly too busy to spend much time worrying about a bloke called Chopper Read, sitting in his cell out at Risdon.

But thankfully someone brought my case to the attention of Michael Hodgman – my lawyer, Anita Betts. Anita and I have had some issues over the years, but I am very grateful to her for doing that.

Once I found out that Michael Hodgman had listened to what Anita had to say and taken my case on, I felt a bit better because I knew that, apart from Andrew

Peacock, Michael didn't back losing causes because he, too, was a very busy man.

As well as everything else, he's a lieutenant commander in the naval reserve. Until his retirement in March this year, he was Her Majesty's Shadow Attorney-General in Tasmania. Well, that's what it said on his business card. He's a real monarchist.

Poor bugger has emphysema now but reckons, even though he's in his seventies, that he'll continue to work as a barrister. There will be some lucky crims in Tasmania who will really benefit from having Michael Hodgman as their lawyer.

I know he worked his guts out to get me out of Risdon, and to get rid of the Dangerous Criminals Act. He took my appeal against the guilty verdict for shooting Sidney Michael Collins all the way to the Full Bench of the High Court and only lost it three to two.

He is an extraordinarily eloquent man, something I tried to get across when I wrote a poem about him called 'The Mouth from the South'.

I don't know if he read it the first time it was published. So, with kind permission from me, it is reprinted here.

THE MOUTH FROM THE SOUTH

From Queenstown to Hobart Town,
From Canberra to Darling Downs,
He fought a thousand battles,
In a hundred different towns,
And while he's very sober,

And always in good condition,
He's a soap box battler,
A dinkum Aussie politician,
And while most just call him Michael,
When they're drunk they call him Mick,
They know the Mouth from the South
Will never miss a trick.
The champion of the underdog,
And the drinking man's friend,
He'll start a fight then finish it,
And take it to the end,
And when it comes to trouble, boy,
He don't ever run and hide,
And when your back's against the wall,
You'll find him at your side,
And when the Devil comes a-knocking,
He'll stick there to the end,
And I am proud I even shook his hand,
He's the Aussie battler's friend.

Michael's gift with words was legendary before I immortalised him in rhyme. The story goes that, when the High Court was hearing my case, a bloke by the name of Damian Bugg, the Commonwealth Director of Public Prosecutions, bet Michael that he – The Buggster, as I called him – wouldn't even be asked to address the court. Basically, he was implying that my case was so weak, the judges would just listen to Michael Hodgman QC MP's submission, then decide against us.

But after Michael spoke, and spoke so well, on my behalf to the Full Bench of the High Court, surprise,

surprise – The Buggster was asked to address them. And after Damian Bugg had finished, Michael was given the right of reply. A lot of seasoned lawyers in Melbourne, where the case was heard, said they'd never seen anything like it. The judges were highly impressed by what Michael Hodgman said on my behalf, even though, in the end, they decided not to grant me leave to appeal.

I paid a lot of money to lawyers to get my case to the High Court, but Michael Hodgman did all that work for me for nothing. A truly amazing man.

I seem to remember him giving me a bit of advice along the way.

'Mark,' he said, 'you'll never get out of prison unless you marry someone from Tasmania.'

How was I going to get married to someone in Tasmania – or anywhere – when I was in jail? And, anyway, it all sounded like something from the convict days, marrying into the local landed gentry to get out of jail. These days, Michael reckons he never said this, but he agrees that he did give me the introduction that led to me meeting the woman who would become my first wife, Mary-Ann Hodge.

Michael knew Mary-Ann because she was one of the Golding family, and if you know Hobart, you'll know that the Goldings have a big jewellery shop in Liverpool Street. In fact, the Goldings go right back to 1858, when William Golding arrived in Hobart and became an apprentice watchmaker. Michael knew Bruce Golding OBE through horse racing.

Mary-Ann's own parents were pretty wealthy too. Ernie Vincent Hodge, Mary-Ann's father, was born a millionaire. The family had a bit of bad luck with money over the years, the fortune getting whittled down from time to time, but the Hodges were always asset rich even when they were cash poor. They had a huge country estate, filled to overflowing with priceless antiques, and farm sheds filled with priceless, famous old cars, such as a 1937 Chevy and Mark 1 Jags. They lived in a grand house just off Grasstree Hill Road, on 500 acres of good farmland, and all this is even before we get to Glen Air, another farming property of 250 acres with another large house on it. That had been owned by Mary-Ann's grandmother. So, the whole family is pretty rich and very much part of the Tasmanian aristocracy. Mary-Ann was a member of the Jaguar Car Club, which, I suppose, also made her a member of the landed gentry.

Mary-Ann worked in the tax office and, I guess at Michael's suggestion, started writing to me in Risdon Prison. Her family's place is called Talbot Lodge and when she wrote to me the first time, in 1994, I didn't bother writing back because I saw the address and thought Talbot Lodge was a mental hospital. Then she wrote to me again and by that time I had worked out that Talbot Lodge might be not a mental hospital but her home.

In fact, Talbot Lodge has a pretty famous place in the history of Australian horse racing. It is where Piping Lane was born and bred, in 1966. Piping Lane was a gelding that won the Melbourne Cup in 1972 at forty to one. He had a bit of a career racing in Tasmania and was then bought for $6000 by a bloke named Ray Trinder and sent across to Victoria, where George Hanlon trained him with a view to winning the Cup.

He was a bit different as a horse trainer, was George Hanlon. He could murder the English language and once said, 'I don't mind losing, I just hate getting beaten.' I can relate to that.

When one of his horses was beaten, he would explain to the disappointed owners, 'Well, horses are only human, you know.' He certainly tried to treat them that way, believing that horses shouldn't be kept in stables in the inner city. He had a property out the back of Geelong, where he trained his horses and let them swim in the sea while he chased them around in an old white jeep. He had the speedo of the jeep recalibrated so he could measure just how fast his horses were going.

His training methods certainly worked with Piping Lane, much to the surprise of a lot of people, including his Melbourne Cup jockey, Johnny Letts. Letts was from South Australia and had not ridden at Flemington before. When he was asked about Piping Lane's chances of winning the Melbourne Cup in 1972, he said he was only there to make up the numbers.

Piping Lane was then only the third Tasmanian-bred horse to win the Melbourne Cup and he beat at least one real champion on the first Tuesday in September that year, as Gunsynd, the Goondiwindi Grey, was third.

After I worked out that Talbot Lodge wasn't a mental institution but a horse-breeding establishment of some standing, I wrote back to Mary-Ann and it turned out we had a bit in common. Her parents were Seventh Day Adventists and my parents were too, even though my father, Keith Alfred Read, had by this time ceased to be one.

So, we kept writing to each other and at some stage it must have become a bit of a problem for her boyfriend. One day, while they were in Scotland, they had an argument about me. The boyfriend dumped her out of the car . . . in Scotland. It's a long way to walk home from Scotland. And a book got thrown at her – one of my books.

Anyway, she decided not to be pushed around by this boyfriend and that she would come and meet me at Risdon Prison.

She fell in love with me as soon as she saw me. How could you blame her? She was a rather rotund woman, Mary-Ann. But she loved me.

One thing led to another and, in 1995, we were married in the prison library. Michael Hodgman QC MP was my best man.

We were married for a few years while I was still in jail. Then came my release. Michael came through for me on his promise that he would get the Dangerous Criminals Act brought before the Houses of Parliament in Tasmania to have the legislation taken out of the hands of the governor and full cabinet and returned to the Supreme Court.

Under the new law, I couldn't be kept in prison indefinitely just because somebody thought I might reoffend. I had to have a set penalty for my crime of shooting Sidney Michael Collins. I was given five years and nine months. I could have got out earlier, on parole, but I told them to stick their parole up their bums. I didn't want to have to live by all their petty, bureaucratic parole rules. So, I got out after five years and nine months, and went to live with Mary-Ann on Glen Air, which by this time her parents had given to her.

Shortly after his youngest daughter married the infamous criminal and author Mark Brandon 'Chopper' Read, Ernie Hodge had a massive stroke. It left him paralysed down the left-hand side of his body, but he recovered enough to continue with one of his favourite pastimes – a visit each November to the antique motor show in Ballarat. They love their cars, the Hodges, and Mary-Ann was no exception.

The day I got out of Risdon was pretty hilarious. Mary-Ann picked me up in her Jaguar. The media was chasing us as we drove. So, there was all 120 kilos of her with her driving gloves on, in her XJ6 Jaguar, and she was really loving it. She was going at 160 kilometres per hour along these little dirt back roads in Tasmania.

We pulled up and spoke to the media only once. The journalist was a lady reporter; I can't remember her name but she seemed quite harmless, so I had a chat with her.

Eventually we got to Glen Air and I was getting prepared to settle into the life of a country squire. The funny thing was that Glen Air was on the same road as Risdon Prison, Grasstree Hill Road. The Hobart Dogs Home is also in that area. I know a few prisoners who would have fitted in well there. An even funnier thing is that in February 2010 they announced they were sending dogs to Risdon Prison. Three labrador pups will be trained by the prisoners to assist people in wheelchairs. At one end of Grasstree Hill Road, then, you had Risdon and at the other you had the town of Richmond, with its old convict jail, which they reckon is Australia's oldest prison. It is five years older than Port Arthur. So, in between Risdon and this relic of the convict days, you had Glen Air, which I didn't know when Mary-Ann first took me there in her Jag was going to become my little prison farm.

I think the police would have preferred me to be back in Risdon, or even in the dark old convict cell at Richmond. I hadn't had my freedom for long when they came to arrest me for possession of a hand gun. Someone who was trying to set me up sent pictures to Robbie Jarvis, who was in Risdon Prison, of me aiming a hand gun at a lamppost. The police confiscated the photographs and said, 'Read has got a hand gun.' I was charged on the strength of these photographs.

It cost me $5000 to hire Michael Hodgman to argue that the photos couldn't be used as evidence that I had possession of a hand gun. It was a replica hand gun. That was my story, anyway. Thanks to Michael Hodgman QC MP, I was found not guilty. That was the only time he charged me for his legal services.

There were a few other things waiting for me when I got out of prison – ten grand in the same safety deposit box that the gun had been kept in, and another $10,000, hidden in a vacuum cleaner pipe. That had come from the money I had in Anita Betts's trust account, which I had asked her to give to Mary-Ann for when I got out.

She somehow managed to get through a lot of my money, did Mary-Ann. The farmhouse at Glen Air was rat-infested and needed rewiring and painting. I spent

$5000 just getting the place rewired. Mary-Ann always wanted to be spending money on the place. She would spend the money before we even had it. One of the mistakes I made while I was still in prison was to give her power of attorney over my money. She went through money like a packet of salts.

I eventually got Mary-Ann to sign the power of attorney back to me, but only after a struggle. She argued that I might end up behind bars again and that she might need to lay her hands on money quickly. She was one of the people who convinced me to sign over my rights to the movie *Chopper* to promoter Michael Gudinski. That was another big mistake that has cost me a lot of money, and something else we will get to later on.

I probably went through a bit of money myself at the casino in Hobart, which was where we ended up the first night after I was released. And there was one night at a certain men's club when I was apparently the life of the party. I had gone into town to buy Mary-Ann a birthday present but had got distracted. They call Hobart 'Slowbart' but things were very pacy and racy that night; I think a bouncer or two might have urged me to settle down a bit. And I was carrying someone – it seems, a very attractive, scantily clad young woman – around on my shoulders for a while.

All good fun.

But back out at Glen Air, once the roaring hangover disappeared, it was all very peaceful and rural. And it was all a bit different for a boy who grew up in suburban Melbourne and behind the walls of Pentridge.

Mary-Ann and I used to get the water trucked in and pumped into the concrete tanks for seventy-five dollars a week. That was the drinking water. If a possum got into the drinking water and drowned, this would foul it, so you had to get the possum out and get more fresh water trucked in. We put the dead possums in the septic tank because when they rotted, they produced bacteria that would eat the poo. But the possums would also block the septic tanks, so you would have to get down in those and clean them out too.

If I wasn't cleaning out the septic tanks, I was cleaning up after Mary-Ann's two fox terriers, Ronnie and Reggie. Now, you shouldn't have a pair of fighting fox terriers anywhere near sheep. But at Glen Air we had sheep properties on three sides of us. On one of those sides was Mary-Ann's parents' place. They had sheep as well as horses. When Ronnie and Reggie were let off their leashes, they would run like the wind until they were out of sight. Then they would reappear covered in fresh blood.

Mary-Ann knew what they had been doing – attacking sheep – but begged me not to report them or tell her dad. As if I'd do that. I've never been a dobber. A dobber is a dog, so that kind of makes dobbing in dogs even worse. Well, that's what I thought then.

But things changed a fair bit when Reggie and Robbie took care of my favourite pet mother hen, Gloria Swanson. She lived in the hen house right next to the dog yard in which we kept Reggie and Ronnie. Gloria Swanson was a large, proud fowl with thirteen little chicks all following her around and going *cheep*

cheep cheep. When she sensed danger, such as a large bird flying over, she would give a distress call and all thirteen chicks would vanish under the protection of her large wings. It was a wonderful display of motherly love, especially to a bloke like me who at that time didn't think he'd had a lot of motherly love.

One day, Reggie and Ronnie dug under the fence separating the dog yard from the chook shed. I found Gloria Swanson with blood all around her backside. She was still alive but I knew I had to put her down. Even as I did, she was still trying to call her chicks to her.

In spite of Mary-Ann's tears of protest, I rang one of the farm workers, Paul Manning, and told him to come and bring his .22 calibre rifle, as I needed him to shoot Ronnie and Reggie. He arrived within five minutes, and I tied the two dogs to a post and Paul shot them both through the left eye. They both went out like a light.

I dug a large hole and put the two dogs in it, then filled it, not with earth but with quick drying cement because I didn't want it to be dug up by some other animal. The cement took about fifteen minutes to dry. As soon as it did, Mary-Ann fell on the grave and cried and cried.

I think it was that night that our son, Charlie, was conceived. Mary-Ann had stopped taking the pill after we had begun living together, and eight and a half months after Ronnie and Reggie were shot, Charlie Vincent Read was born. I named him Charlie after a dear friend of mine from Melbourne, Mad Charlie, who had rung up out of the blue just the day before.

I don't regret having little Charlie; he's a lovely little boy and I love him very much. He's going to a good school in Hobart, and I still go and see him about once a year.

Another thing I had to do a lot of at Glen Air, besides cleaning out septic tanks, was chop wood. We had tonnes of wood shipped to the paddock near the house and I had to cut it up with a chain saw. I got a certificate in chain saw operation while I was in prison, so I knew what I was doing. Our house had five fireplaces and it was my job to keep them all going. Mary-Ann always wanted the house to be warm – as warm as toast, she would say. It was very cold down there in Tasmania, so I was constantly cutting bloody wood.

Soon after Charlie was born, I crashed a car into an irrigation pipe. When I got out of the car, I put my foot into an irrigation hole and broke my ankle. I had to walk nearly two kilometres back to the farm-house, falling on my face with every step I took. And I was falling into mud all the time because it was raining.

When I got back to the house, a BBC television crew was there to meet me. They wanted to chat about life on the farm or whatever. They always want to talk to you about something, the media. But that day, it was insane. I was in so much pain, and covered in mud, and I have no idea what they said to me. I remember that they did ask me why I was hobbling. I just thought I had a sprained ankle. They must have thought I was some sort of mad hillbilly, covered in mud and hobbling.

That evening, I had to get taken to hospital. My foot was now so swollen, it was coming out of my boot. I told them I thought I had only twisted my ankle, but no, they were the experts and it was broken. They operated on me, put me in plaster and returned me to the farm.

I still had to cut the wood, hobbling along with the chain saw, can of two-stroke petrol and the wheelbarrow. One day as I hobbled up the hill, I got bitten by a bloody baby tiger snake on the ankle that I hadn't broken. I hobbled back down, still carrying the chain saw and can of two-stroke petrol, climbed the fence, and by the time I got to the back door, felt like a man who was very drunk. It felt like my stomach was empty, and I needed a big drink of water. When I had one, I spewed it up.

I lay down in the heat of the kitchen and went to sleep until Mary-Ann found me.

She said, 'What's the matter?'

I said, 'I think I've been bitten by a snake.'

I went to the hospital and was given antivenom. Then, after I got home and was pretty soon out chopping wood again, I got bitten on the back of my thumb by a white-tail spider that had crawled into my glove. It had died as I'd rolled the glove over my thumb, but not before biting me. The antivenom from the tiger snake treatment helped a bit with the white-tail spider poison, but I scratched the bite for three years and it used to rot away the skin. The tiger snake bite after-effects lasted about seven years; the skin around it used to rot away and I would scratch it and scratch it.

Anyway, by now I was thinking this so-called quiet life in the Tasmanian countryside wasn't really for me.

My nickname was Chopper, not Woodchopper. The last straw came when I was cleaning out the septic tank and got bitten by a scorpion. And I looked up from shovelling the shit, with this bloody scorpion bite, and there was Mary-Ann above me with little Charlie, saying her mum and dad wanted a tonne of wood chopped. So I said yeah, chopped the wood and took it over to their house and left it at the back door.

I poked my head in to tell them it was there. All they said was 'Could you close the door on the way out?' That was it.

I went back to Mary-Ann and said, 'Can you drive me to the airport?'

She sullenly drove me to the airport. When we got there, she asked me, 'Where are you going?'

I said, 'Collingwood.'

She said, 'I knew it. Will you come back?'

I said, 'No, never!'

Mary-Ann said, 'So, this is it, then?'

She didn't even bother to get out of the car to give me a hug goodbye.

I said, 'You're going to have to find someone else to chop the wood and clean out the septic tank.'

Before turning on my heel and walking off into the night, I kissed Charlie on the cheek. I said to him, 'I will see you later, you poor little bugger – I love you, son.'

I do love Charlie, with all my heart.

I had a mercenary attitude towards his poor mother, I'm afraid. But I guess she had a pretty mercenary approach to me too.

I sometimes wonder if she ever expected me to get out of Risdon. When I was offered parole towards the end of my sentence, I knocked it back. I think Mary-Ann was quietly relieved about that because it gave her a bit of time to get herself sorted. It also gave her a bit of time to sort a few things out for me – my safety deposit box and my guns.

I wasn't allowed to have a gun – it would have been a breach of the conditions of my release. Mary-Ann could have a gun licence, though, which meant we could go and visit gun clubs and shoot at targets to our hearts' content.

I didn't love Mary-Ann, but I did trust her with a list of things I wouldn't trust many others with, believe me – my guns and my safety deposit box prominent among them. However, when I came back to Victoria I only had $300 in my pocket and the clothes I stood up in. When I chopped that last tonne of wood, I had also just spent my last five grand on getting the house rewired. So, I was broke.

It's a funny thing: a few weeks before I left Tasmania, ABC television had done a feature on Mary-Ann, Charlie and me for *Australian Story*. Now they had somehow got wind that I might be going back to Melbourne, to Margaret Cassar, which, of course, would put a big hole in their show, which was all about the infamous Chopper Read living the blissful life of the country squire in Tasmania.

They rang Margaret to see what was happening. She wouldn't tell them anything. *60 Minutes* also rang her and wanted to know what was going on. Again, she didn't tell them anything. Margaret doesn't like the media much. She doesn't like having a high profile either, which is why her decision to help me write this book is interesting.

Margaret has had lots of offers to tell her story to the media, but she's left it all for this book. I think you will like what she has to say.

On this night in June 2001, Margaret came to meet me at Tullamarine airport. She said I looked as mad as a cut snake – or a real Tasmanian nuff nuff – when I got off the plane. I was taking twelve milligrams of Xanax, a highly addictive anti-anxiety medicine, a day. That's enough to kill a brown dog.

'You want to come off that rubbish,' Margaret said.

She took me off it immediately, not knowing it was an addictive benzodiazepine drug. Three weeks after I came off it, my head felt like it was going to explode, due to withdrawal symptoms. I knew I also had hepatitis C, and I was drinking heavily, despite my bad liver, so I eventually got into a taxi and asked to be taken to St Vincent's Hospital.

'Drive quickly,' I said to the driver, 'I think I am going to die.'

He drove on the footpath, raced through lights; he did all sorts of things to speed up the journey. A black man from the Sudan, he kept saying, 'You won't die today, brother,' and invoking the name of Allah.

I am not a religious person – growing up in the Seventh Day Adventist Church cured me of that. But at that stage I would have accepted help from anyone and if this Sudanese taxi driver needed help from Allah to help me, then praise be to Allah!

At St Vincent's I gave the emergency department my name. And then everything went blank.

When I woke up, every bone in my body was aching. They said I had had a seizure and collapsed in the foyer in the emergency ward; that I was shaking and then my whole body went stiff.

I've had a number of these seizures since. It turns out I am the sort of person who needs a lot of looking after.

Thank goodness for Margaret, this girl I had first met in the fish and chip shop in Lalor more than twenty years ago; who had written to me when I was in Pentridge; who had agreed to come to Tasmania with me; who I had told to go back to Melbourne to start a new life without me; who had finally said I could come back to Melbourne.

I say 'finally' because, when I first got out of jail, I had indicated to her that I would come back to Melbourne. I rang her the day I got out of Risdon and it was nice to hear her voice. But what she had to say this time wasn't quite as nice as I had hoped. I asked her if I could come back to Melbourne to be with her, and she said she was living with a washing machine salesman, and that life was pretty good for her and not to come back. She said I had made my bed and had to lie in it.

She was pretty pissed off about Mary-Ann and me having a baby. These days Margaret is very accepting of him and so is my other son, Roy, who happily talks about his half-brother Charlie who lives in Tasmania.

But at that stage, Margaret was pretty pissed off about the marriage and the baby.

The other reason Margaret said not to come back was that she was going on a holiday to Malta. She tells me now that she was going to have that holiday, no matter what.

Margaret must have done a bit of thinking in Malta. When she came back, she told me the washing machine salesman was on the way out, and so, when I made that phone call from Hobart airport and asked if it was all right to come back, she said those two beautiful words, 'Bloody oath!'

And they were soon to be followed by two more beautiful words: 'I do!'

CHAPTER 2

MEET MARGARET READ, NEE CASSAR

Y ou're probably wondering what sort of person falls
in love with a bloke like Mark Brandon 'Chopper'
Read who has a criminal record as long as his tattooed
arm. And then sticks with him, one way or another, for
nearly thirty years.

I wonder about it a lot too. All I can say is that I
am lucky. I love Margaret Cassar, who is now Margaret
Read.

I proposed to her on Channel Ten. One of the benefits
of being Chopper Read is that the media likes to interview
me. Well, it's not always beneficial for everyone –
ask Elle McFeast. But this time it was beneficial for
Margaret and me.

When I first returned to Melbourne, Channel Ten wanted to interview me about why I had come back. Margaret is never really that happy about me talking to the media, and she wasn't happy on this night when she came home and found I'd gone. But I had left a note for her on the table, saying to watch the Channel Ten news at five o'clock. And when the reporter asked me why I had come back to Melbourne, I said, 'I've come back to marry Margaret Cassar.'

That's how I proposed to her. Pretty romantic, eh?

I reckoned that since I had known her all those years from when we met in the fish and chip shop in Lalor, and she'd stuck with me through Pentridge, and then Risdon and everything else – well, we'd be all right married.

So we got married and, as I said in the introduction to this book, Margaret and our son, Roy Brandon Read, are the reason I am writing another book.

I write with a pen on foolscap paper. That's how I got started writing while I was in Pentridge; I used to write in my cell by the light of the television back then. No computer for me, even now that I am out.

I sit at the kitchen table with my pen and pad. While I have been doing this, Margaret's been down the other end of the house on her computer, writing some of her thoughts that, let me tell you, she is now very keen to share. And, after thirty years of putting up with me, I reckon she's earned a chance to have her say.

MARGARET: I have only chosen to write and share my part of this story for the sake of our beautiful son, Roy, so he can gain a better understanding of who his parents, especially his father, are. I didn't want the movie *Chopper* or all the media reports about Mark to answer the questions he may have as he gets older, especially if his parents aren't around to answer them.

My life with Mark has been a journey of mixed emotions and adventures: happy times, sad times, with major interruptions and setbacks, yet with very memorable moments. And I certainly would not have it any other way. It is my journey.

My relationship with Mark seemed to have a mind of its own and my heart followed, even when there were times I didn't want to go back down that same road. Somehow, we managed to get back together, and I can honestly say we've got through it all and made it safely to the other side.

The love I have for Mark has never altered since the day we met. I am married to an amazing man and a gentle man (yes, that's right, a gentle man) and that is the only way I know him to be.

Both Mark and I came from the northern suburbs of Melbourne. I grew up in Epping and he lived in Thomastown, two suburbs away, and we used to get our fish and chips from the same shop, which was run by Alex Marcou, who played for Carlton in the early 1980s. One day, Mark pushed in ahead of me and I said to him, 'My flake's been cooking for a while,' and he replied, 'I am sure it has!'

That's how we met the first time.

I lived in Epping for nineteen years. I moved out to Collingwood when my mother died.

Both my parents were from Malta and emigrated to Australia in the 1950s. They were process workers. Unlike so many of the Maltese who came out then, Mum chose not to live in the western suburbs.

I was fortunate not to have overly strict parents, unlike a lot of other children of European migrants back then. I was able to have friends and socialise from an early age. Both my parents were very sociable and I can remember there were always people coming around to visit, as we blended in well with the Aussies. Epping was a small town and everyone did know everyone, so that made it easier. Of course, my parents had rules that both my brother, Ron, and I had to abide by. My mother's rules were . . . never be a stickybeak, and that if you asked questions about people, not to repeat anything that you were told. She also said to treat people as you find them, no matter who they are or what their background might be, and to be yourself and have a mind of your own.

I have never forgotten that and I always do treat people as I find them. As well, I have learned to stand on my own two feet. Nothing gets in the way of my decisions, and no one can persuade me to do anything I don't want to do.

I'm a very earthy person, and can and do socialise in all circles. I don't ask personal questions and tend to want that in return, as I am very protective of my personal life. I have a bit of a short fuse, which comes naturally to me, being Maltese. We put a lot of work into ourselves, and into our relationships, and do so with passion and pride. I don't recommend upsetting someone with a Maltese background.

Maybe it was those fine qualities that drew Mark and me together. I would like to think that.

When I moved to Collingwood in 1979, I lived with Mum's brother, my Uncle Charlie. After he died, in 1994, he left me the house that Mark, Roy and I now live in. Mark has done a wonderful job renovating this house.

I want very much to dedicate what I write here to Roy Brandon Read, and if he is the only one who reads my story – well, I have to be happy with that, as it is an achievement in itself.

Mark and Roy, I love you both with all my heart and I treasure our little family.

CHAPTER 3

THE EARLY DAYS

I was born on 17 November 1954, in the Carlton Women's Maternity Hospital. At the time, my father, Keith Alfred Read, was based at the Balcombe army barracks on the Mornington Peninsula, so I was brought home to a log cabin in Mount Martha.

Well, that's what my mother and father told me. But I have no memory of it. My first memory is of being in the hallway in a house in Thomastown with my mother, who had just got out of the bath. She was naked. It was the most shocking sight I have ever seen and haunts me to this day. I saw this naked woman standing in the light and it just scared me, I don't know why. It might have been the light, it might have been something else, but it just scared me.

The other thing I remember about my early days was that there was a lot of religion. My mother was a Seventh Day Adventist and we got taken to church all the time. I was forced to pray on my knees. If I opened my eyes when I was praying, I got smacked. I got smacked for this and I got smacked for that. If I did anything wrong at church, I got smacked. It was a pretty miserable existence being a Seventh Day Adventist.

From sunset Friday to sunset Saturday, it was the Sabbath; Saturday instead of Sunday, that's why they're called Seventh Day Adventists. They reckon that after God had made the world, and all that therein lies, he took Saturday off instead of Sunday. On the Sabbath, you couldn't watch TV, you couldn't play football or cricket – you couldn't do anything. All you could do was pray and read the Bible, listen to gospel music and praise God. What sort of life is that for a young boy?

My relationship with my mother is good now but has not always been so. My father told me that when I was first brought home from hospital, he found her with a pillow dangerously near me, and that another time, he saw her doing something to me in the bath. He reckoned that when he went to work he'd be worried whether he would still have a son when he came home.

My mother always said my father was mad and I should not believe everything he said. In the last little while, I have come to accept this as the truth.

In April 2010, Margaret, Roy and I travelled to Hobart to catch up with Mum and my sister. It was a wonderful four days. As my mum and I laughed and cried and told lots of stories, I came to believe that my father told me a lot of lies about my mother.

Margaret, Roy and I stayed at Wrest Point, and had a hire car. We would pick Mum up from her retirement home and take her out to do the whole Tasmanian tourism thing, all the time telling stories. We went to the Tahune AirWalk, which is kilometres out into the bush south of Hobart. And another day we went to Salmon Ponds and wondered why it was called this when all the fish in it are trout. Turns out that in the nineteenth century, they brought both salmon and trout eggs, packed in ice, out from Scotland. When they finally got them to Hobart, they took them up to where Salmon Ponds is and put them in the Plenty River. First chance they got, the salmon headed to the ocean and were never seen again. The trout hung around.

We talked a lot about our early days in Thomastown and other places we lived around Melbourne. Mum said that Dad wasn't always as bad as he became in later life. We talked about the fact that he was an orphan and had a tough early life. He was born in Hay in the southern New South Wales outback and abandoned in front of the Hay Nursing Hospital. I don't know who rescued him but a lady called Belle raised him. She died when he was twelve. After that, he had no one to look after him, so went to work on a farm. Then, at sixteen, he enlisted in the army. Enlisting in the army was something I once tried too, but they wouldn't have me. I apparently failed the psychological testing.

Margaret really enjoyed the time with my mum in Tasmania. She has always got on very well with her. My mother once gave Margaret a replica of a Victoria Cross, which has on it the inscription 'For Valour'. Margaret wears it all the time.

Mum is still very religious. She is the daughter of a Seventh Day Adventist minister and her grandfather helped found the church in Australia. Her maiden name was Westlake, her grandfather being Pastor George Westlake. Her sister, Noreen Westlake, married Dr John Knight, who became famous appearing on television on *The Mike Walsh Show* under the name Dr James Wright . He still writes in the newspapers, giving medical advice.

Dr James Wright had $44 million thieved off him by a crooked developer in America. If you have 44 million spare and can invest it in mad developments, you deserve to have it thieved off you. I reckon he'd be down to his last six or seven million now. When I said that to Mum in April, she laughed and said, 'And he's only just stopped talking about it now!'

Dr James Wright once came to dinner at Glen Air with Mary-Ann and me. That's the only time I ever met him, I think. He appeared on the *Australian Story* program about me, and said, 'My view is that he'll stay okay and be my happy, friendly nephew for a long, long time. I hope so.'

Thanks, Doc.

I am told the whole transcript of the *Australian Story* program is still on the program's website. It would probably make interesting reading.

I do remember how the *Australian Story* show finished up. I was quoting Kris Kristofferson, the

American singer/songwriter who had a song that said something along the lines of being a poet, a prophet, a pusher, pilgrim and a problem when stoned. A contradiction – part truth and part fiction. I suppose that sums me up and it sums up a lot of other people, too.

As I said, my old man was a professional soldier, and spent twenty-four years in the army. He fought in World War II, in Korea and in New Guinea. During World War II, he served in New Guinea, New Britain, the Solomons . . . the Pacific region generally. He was in the infantry, so I guess he was at the sharp end of the fighting a fair bit. At the end of the war, he got transferred to the British Commonwealth Occupational Forces and spent two years in Japan.

He told me a lot of stories he reckoned were funny, about the things he and a mate, Bernie Waterhouse, used to get up to when they were guarding prisoners. They would get a bucket and stuff called soft soap and would leave it to sit overnight. Then they would give it to the Japs to use when they went into the surf to lather up; you know how the Japs love to wash themselves. My father told me he and Bernie used to machine-gun them to death in the surf with the Japanese's own Mitsubishi seven-millimetre machine-guns. A lot of people don't know that it was the Mitsubishi people who now make cars who were the biggest manufacturers of guns and small arms in World War II.

Anyway, my father came back into camp and this British Red Cross officer said, 'Where are all your men, Corporal Read?'

My father said, 'They swam away!'

The British Red Cross officer said, 'Well, they will come back when they are hungry.'

When the prisoners were found floating dead in the surf, the British Red Cross officer wanted my father and Bernie court-martialled. It went all the way up to Major-General 'Red Robbie' Robertson, who issued an order that the matter was to be heard internally, at a company level, and that there was to be no court martial or mention of the word murder. He said no Australian soldier had been shown to be guilty of murder since Breaker Morant.

I asked my father what, since it was wartime, was all the fuss about. But at that point, the war had been over for eight weeks. My father told me the Australian soldiers killed more Japanese in that first eight weeks after the war ended than in the war itself. When they found out what the Japs had done to Australian soldiers at, for example, the Burma Railway, they were wild.

One day, my old man saw a Jap captain sharpening a samurai sword. General Douglas MacArthur had issued an order that if you saw anyone with a samurai sword, you had to shoot him. So, my old man shot him.

The Red Cross officer got involved, again! These Red Cross majors weren't really majors: they were people who had gone to Oxford and Cambridge, and then got a commission in the Red Cross, and a major's badge. They didn't really lead infantry into battle. They could give orders but no one paid any attention to them. Basically, they were there to hand out Red Cross goods.

Anyhow, this British Red Cross major said to my father, 'I am going to charge you with murder, Corporal Read; that man was sharpening that sword for me.'

My old man picked up the sword and said, 'Well, it's mine now and, anyway, I was only following General Douglas MacArthur's order that if you see a Jap with a samurai sword, you shoot him, no questions asked.'

My dad said he had some great fun in Japan . . . but people were playing games with him and the rest of the Australians. The Americans.

After the atomic bombs were dropped on Hiroshima and Nagasaki, the Australians had to rebuild the railway line into Hiroshima. When it was finished, they took the train into the city. The Americans gave the Australians Kodak cameras and said to them, 'Take as many photos of ground zero as you can.' They did this and handed them over to the Americans when they returned.

My father says it was only when the Americans were able to develop the film that they would go in, because then they knew the radiation levels were safe. While they kept getting blank photos back from the Australians, they wouldn't. It was twelve to eighteen weeks before any American people went into Hiroshima. They knew all the time the radiation levels were dangerously high, but didn't share such titbits with the Australians. I wonder how many Australians got cancer because of all that.

My father said he also went into Nagasaki. There he saw Japanese kids with plasma leaking out of their skin. He used to put toilet paper on their skin to stop it.

When he finally came back to Australia from Japan, he joined the merchant navy for two years. I think he got a bit bored with the merchant navy. During the

Korean War, he joined the army again and fought in Korea in 1950. He was out of the army in 1947 and had rejoined it by 1949. Basically, he just didn't like civilian life. After Korea, he went to Malaya for what was called a 'police action'; it was the Australians helping the British.

I guess Mum and Dad got on all right back in those days. To please her, he used to be a Seventh Day Adventist at home, but as soon as he got away from her, he wasn't. He used to take me when he went to work in the army barracks and as soon as he got there, he was swearing like a trooper, which, of course, he was: he'd be saying fuck this and fuck that, and carrying on like a redneck. You wouldn't have thought he was an elder in the Seventh Day Adventist Church. He kept up the charade for a while, but when I left the Seventh Day Adventist Church, he said he wouldn't do it any longer either. I was fifteen when I did this.

I went to twenty-four different schools . . . Thomastown, Thomastown East, Lalor High. We moved around a lot. I got expelled from nearly every school I went to. We were also in Brisbane for two years.

It was when I was at Wellers Hill State School in Melbourne that I was interfered with.

My parents wouldn't walk me to school. An older kid, who was in Form Five, so he was about sixteen or so, would take a group of us to school in the morning and then walk us home in the afternoon. He used to stop off in the park on the way, and would take one kid at a time off into the bushes and do something to them.

He took me into the bushes and stuck his dick up my bum, and I told him I didn't like that and I was going to tell on him. He told me not to. On the way home, I pooed my pants.

I set fire to St Barnabas church that night. My old man pulled me out from under the church, which was across the road from where we were living. He yelled at me, 'What are you doing?' I don't remember what I said then, but me doing this was probably some sort of reaction to what had happened with the kid. I don't remember much about him. I know he was a Seventh Day Adventist, so my mum trusted him, and that he lived up the road from us. I didn't see much of him after that.

We went to live in Brisbane because my grandmother was dying of bowel cancer. My mother went up there to nurse her and my father got a two-year transfer there. When my grandmother died, Mum came back to Thomastown. That was only a year after we went to Brisbane, and Dad had to stay there for another twelve months because he couldn't get a transfer back. When he did, it was to Balcombe army barracks on the Mornington Peninsula.

So, with all this moving around, I got messed around at school. When I went from Wellers Hill School to Mornington School, I had to do Grade Two all over again. Then I had to do Grade Five all over again. Then I went to Lalor High School, then Collingwood High School. After that, I went to Ringwood East Coaching College. It was a school for dumb kids, for kids who had a lot of trouble at school. I wasn't much of an academic.

I used to get bullied a lot at school too. They never said why they picked on me; they just didn't like me, I guess. They used to wait for me after school and take turns kicking my head in. It was very hurtful.

I finally left school in Form Two of high school, but they had to bodgie up my paperwork so I could. I had really only done Form One but you couldn't leave until you had finished Form Two, so they gave me a false grading.

One of the first jobs I got was as a nightclub bouncer at a place called the Mae West. The reason I got this job was that I knew a bloke called Johnny Harris. I met him at the Try Boys youth club in Prahran, where I used to go to wrestle. Johnny Harris could fight very well and was a good bouncer. He said he wouldn't work for them at the Mae West unless I did too.

I used to get a dollar an hour and Johnny got five dollars an hour. I wasn't a nightclub bouncer's backside back then. But then Johnny Harris taught me to fight.

He would say, 'You just stand there and I will throw punches at you and you just punch back.' I got used to punches to the face and punched him back, and that's how he taught me to fight.

Then, after that job, I didn't do much at all. I did go to work for three weeks on my uncle's cane farm at Mossman in Queensland, and blew the clutch out of a Massey Ferguson tractor. Now, you can't blow the clutch out of a Massey Ferguson tractor, but I did. I would rev the thing up, and take my foot off the clutch and lift the front wheels, and this amused me so much, I just kept on doing it and eventually blew the clutch. My uncle said no one could blow the clutch of a Massey Ferguson tractor, and he sacked me.

There's another member of my family I should talk about. I have a sister, Deborah, who is eleven months younger than me. She left the Seventh Day Adventist Church and became a born again Christian, and worked in Odessa, Russia, for a while helping repatriate Jews to Israel. She wrote to me when she was there and said she could talk in tongues. I replied that, 'Seeing you are living in Odessa, Russia, that would be pretty handy.' She didn't write back for a while because she thought I was taking the mickey out of her. Well, I was, I suppose.

Deborah also used to live on an all-female right-wing Christian kibbutz in Israel. When they weren't picking oranges and grapefruits, they were donning paramilitary uniforms and going to the Golan Heights and taking pot-shots at Arabs who lived there. They used to consider it great fun.

My sister is about five foot eleven and well built. She does judo and karate, is very healthy, doesn't drink or smoke, and is, overall, a very forceful woman.

Deborah was once escorted off stage when she was addressing a private girls school in Tasmania, where she lives now. She was there to talk about violence against women and said to the girls, 'If you are bashed by your husband, get up at three am, get a baseball bat and cave his head in.' She was applauded as she was being led from the stage.

My sister has three children of her own: two sons and a daughter. Her relationship with Mum is on again, off again, all to do with religion. They are talking at the moment, though. Her relationship with me has also been an on-off one, but things are good between us now.

I guess we never really wanted for things as kids. There was food on the table, clothes on our backs, the bills were paid. My old man always had staff sergeant's pay and we lived in a war service home when we were in Thomastown.

Gee, hasn't that place changed since I was a kid? It's like a third-world bomb shelter now. When I was growing up in Thomastown, it was a lovely place, still very rural. The farmers used to drive their cows down the road between the Goodyear Tyre Factory and the houses on the other side of it. There were a lot of Germans there, who set up the Pura dairy. There were also a lot of other immigrants moving in – Italians, Greeks, Macedonians, and, obviously, at least one Maltese family: the Cassars, who moved to Epping.

The Thomastown school that I went to opened in 1961. We walked there along unmade roads; the gutters were just ditches that had water rats coming out of them.

We had an outside dunny until 1969. I didn't see a shower until 1969, when we moved from Thomastown to Prahran. We grew up with a bath. Mum would fill it and go first, then Deborah, then Dad, and I had the bath last. We had to do it that way because hot water was so precious; we had a Briquette hot water service, I remember. When I first saw our shower, I thought, 'This is luxury, this is beautiful!'

I remember Christmas was a pretty boring affair, no matter where we were living. I used to get items of clothing as presents but there was never much in the way of festivities. Mum didn't believe in the celebratory side of Christmas. We were told the celebrations were pagan and they didn't believe in them, and only followed them to please us kids. They reckoned Easter was a pagan celebration too. They are a miserable lot of boring people, the Seventh Day Adventists.

I had a dog called Noddy, a beautiful little Australian terrier. He was really my father's dog. My old man would tie him up and if anyone else tried to untie him, Noddy would go for them. And you couldn't touch him when he was eating. When my dad left my mum, he asked her to look after Noddy for a week until he could come back and get him. When he did, he said, 'Where's the dog?'

She said, 'He's gone, I had him put down.' Dad sat on the back stairs, and cried and cried. I guess I was about sixteen at the time.

The reason Mum and Dad split up was pretty simple. My dad was barking mad, there's no use denying it. I guess that in the end it all got too much for Mum.

Dad would sit at the end of my bed and say to me, 'You know your mother's a lesbian, son.' Who wants to hear that from his father? He would tell me these vivid stories about how my mum was a lesbian because she wouldn't have sex with him.

He used to sleep with a Bentley pump action shotgun in his bed. I saw his madness when I went to live with him after he separated from my mother. I would get up in the night to go to the toilet and would hear the click of the gun and him saying, 'Who goes there?' And I would say, 'It is only me, Dad.'

Once I forgot to say it was me when he said, 'Who goes there?' The next time he really yelled it, so I said, 'It's me,' and it's a good thing I did because he was about to pull the bloody trigger.

I guess you could put all this down to war damage and stress. They'd call it post-traumatic stress disorder today. He never got any help for it; he would have laughed at you if you had suggested that. No, there was nothing wrong with my father or with anyone in his age bracket who had served in the war – they didn't need help.

He died when he was eighty-one. It was sad to see him in his later years, as his memory and health started to fail him. He even began to forget some of the really great things he would say to me when I was living with him in South Yarra in 1977.

He was a very caring parent in his own way. When we were in South Yarra, before I would go out – around midnight – he would have all my clothes neatly ironed for me. I would put them on, and put my overcoat on over the top, Melbourne having a particularly cool climate. Overcoats were also handy for hiding my tools, which Dad would help me assemble before I went out. These were my guns and my knuckle dusters. He had this funny thing of calling knuckle dusters 'knuckle busters'. I could never explain to him that that's not how they worked, though he might have worked it out when he got belted with a set of knuckle dusters one night, something else we will get to later on.

As I would be leaving the house he would say, 'Okay, son, you can't be too careful in your line of business. Don't get into any trouble.' Dad had just helped me put on all my guns and there he was saying, 'Don't get into any trouble!' What else would I be doing?

Dad did know what 'knucklehead' meant. He used to call me that all the time.

Towards the end of his life, he not only couldn't remember those good times we used to have as father and son, I had to be very careful what I did tell him when he came to visit me in Risdon, because he would just go out and tell everyone in the street what we had talked about.

Dad had had a tough life; he had served his country well in times of war and peace. I was very sad when he died; I hope he is resting in peace. I loved my dad very much.

I used to say the jury was still out on my mum but, after that wonderful trip to Tasmania recently, the jury is back. NOT GUILTY.

My father told me that when I was born, Mum held me in her arms and said, 'He's not a gift from God and he will be trouble till the day he dies.'

When I was an infant, I spent a lot of time in a babies home, after Mum got pregnant eight weeks after my birth. Another thing Mum did was put me into a mental institution, the Royal Park Mental Hospital, when I was fifteen years old. She did that because I had left the Seventh Day Adventist Church. Her thinking was that if I was declared insane, I could still go to heaven because God wouldn't punish you if you were insane. The psychiatrists who signed the certification order to put me into Royal Park were both Seventh Day Adventists Mum had taken me to.

While I was in Royal Park, it was my job to clean out the toilet and showers. They had these beautiful white-tiled urinals and six white-tiled bath units. The bath units had wooden tops, which would lock people into the units, which would then be filled with hot or cold water. They were like stocks, these wooden tops, but I was told they didn't use them much.

There was an old Italian man who was also in Royal Park. I called him 'Giovanno from Milano' because his name was Giovanno. I called one of the characters in my adult fairytale Giovanno from Milano. The Giovanno in Royal Park would pat the top of his head as he walked past and I would pat the top of my head back to him.

One day I walked into the bathroom to clean the floor and there he was, lying in a pool of blood. He had cut every vein and artery in his body. There was three foot of blood around him and it had coagulated.

I didn't call anybody. I just started to clean up the blood. I used my mop and hot water, and when the water was blood red, I tipped it out and got some more. I mopped up all the blood except for a two-inch track around Giovanno's body. He looked like he was Mr Bean having landed in the middle of a white-tiled floor. I then cleaned the toilets and went back into the day room.

About twenty minutes later, some doctors and orderlies started making a lot of noise. They weren't talking much about this bloke who had committed suicide. Rather, they were talking about who had done the marvellous cleaning job.

Someone said, 'It was young Read, the one they call Chopper.'

That was when they started giving me shock treatment.

The treatments were supposed to leave you groggy for days but I'd wake up twenty minutes after them, full of energy, like they had injected methamphetamine up my arse. I would want to run around and play handball, and talk at 100 miles an hour. So, they started doing it to me every two or three days, and I had sixty in six months.

How I got out of Royal Park Mental Hospital is interesting. I was being held on a certification order that was only valid as long as I stayed in the grounds of the hospital. That was because it was only signed by two psychiatrists. Once I got onto public property, they couldn't bring me back without an order signed by a judge.

They could do anything they liked to keep me there, and they did. I was put in a secure ward when I got there. It had locked windows with wire on them, and they tied you into your bed at nighttime. I would lie there in a dormitory full of people screaming and shouting, a fifteen-year-old boy with all these nutcases.

One day, my old man said to me, 'Just get onto the public street and I will drive you home.' It had taken him six months to work that out, and I was a bit pissed off about it. But that's what I did and he took me home.

Mum didn't put me back in Royal Park but I think by now, like with Dad, I had just become too much for her.

Margaret has always said that I have been far too tough on my mum in my other books. That's why, as well as organising our recent trip to Tasmania, she persuaded Mum to write something for this book.

Mum was very reluctant to do so, being a very private person herself. She has asked Margaret to ensure that we don't include her full name and I am happy to do that. She has just signed herself 'Mother', which is what she is.

Mark's problem throughout his school life was his inability to adjust in his mind the information the teacher was giving.

For years we engaged tutors for Mark, hoping that one-to-one tuition would help solve his problem. One by one they gave up, not being able to penetrate the barrier they felt was there.

Mark has almost total recall and could remember and recite word for word a conversation or stories that were read to him. However, if there were too many instructions or a sudden change, then it would be confusion – anxiety, disruption. This would have teachers thinking he was insolent – defiant – deliberately obtuse. Punishments physical and verbal would follow.

Year after year it was the same and because his behaviour was so disruptive we were asked to remove him – which we did, from state schools, private schools, special schools, special private schools and high schools. It seemed that no one could help him over his tremendous learning hurdle.

The Federal Education Minister couldn't help.

The Victorian Education Minister couldn't help.

Different councils had nothing in mind.

When Mark was fourteen years of age, we heard of a Dr Humphery, a behavioural scientist just back from America. He saw Mark and assessed him and found that he had no coordination between seeing, hearing and doing. As there were no help-groups or clinics, Dr Humphery was unable to refer Mark on.

At least we knew why, and that helped us to understand the problem and the far-reaching effects it had.

After years of abuse, jeers, sarcasm and taunts, Mark was showing signs of severe disturbance: self-mutilation, night-mares, sleepwalking and running away from home.

In quieter moments he was confiding, funny and caring: a very loving boy.

Then puberty kicked in and Mark exploded with an anger that was palpable. An anger we all felt: classmates, teachers, family.

Because he was told all his life that he was useless, stupid and moronic, this eventually led him on a path that almost destroyed him and those who love him.

Looking back now with Dr Humphery's diagnosis, we know that from the time Mark started school he was distressed and bewildered by a sensory overload he was unable to define.

His teachers, some quite sadistic, were frustrated and exasperated without the knowledge [we] now have to help him.

Underneath the image he presents he is still the loving, gentle, generous and funny man we all love.

My last words – Thank God for Margaret.

Mother

CHAPTER 4

FIGHTING IN THE STREETS

How I went from being my mother's little boy and a practising Seventh Day Adventist to a life of crime, which ended up being turned into a world-famous movie, has always been interesting to a lot of people, I suppose.

At the age of fifteen, I was just fighting in the streets, and one thing led to another. I was a bloody good street fighter because I had one basic rule: when you're fighting Chopper Read, there are no rules.

Ambrose Palmer, the boxing trainer, once described me as a kamikaze fighter. He had been a very good footballer and boxer himself before training Johnny Famechon to become the world featherweight champion. So, I was pretty keen to get some tips from him when I went to his gym out in Footscray. And all he said was that I fought like a kamikaze pilot and that sooner or later, either I or someone else would end up dead. He was right there – and it wasn't me!

All up, I had about twenty fights in the boxing ring, and mostly with blokes who were older and bigger than me. But I managed to hold my own with most of them, even draw a bit of blood. Ambrose Palmer knew I could never be taught the Queensberry Rules. If the other bloke fought dirty, I fought dirtier – right to the death, if necessary. But let's be honest here, I always suspected the other bloke would fight dirty, so went in prepared every time. Get your retaliation in first. I'd go in with hands, feet, elbows and headbutts and would always be looking around for a heavy object. I guess wrestling was really more in my line. I did a bit of that at the Try Boys Club in Prahran.

I always had a lot of time for Ambrose Palmer. He was just nineteen when he won his first national title. He was still working as a blacksmith when he knocked out Jack Haines in Sydney, which gave him the Australian middleweight crown. By the time he had turned twenty-one, Ambrose had also won the national light-heavyweight and heavyweight titles.

He got a bit of a pasting, though, when he took on the American heavyweight Young Stribling, a bloke who managed to go twelve rounds with the German heavyweight champion Max Schmeling. Ambrose was literally and otherwise punching way above his weight in that one. He had to take a break from boxing for a while to recover from that fight and that's when he took up football.

He ended up playing eighty-three games for Footscray in the VFL. He was also a successful professional sprinter, having won the Kyneton Gift sprinting race.

But his greatest gift, and the reason I respected Ambrose Palmer, was his commitment to helping other people. While he wasn't able to rehabilitate me, he did an awful lot for many others.

Ambrose Palmer was there the day of the Great Bookie Robbery in Melbourne in 1976. This little event is now part of Australian folklore because very little of the money was ever recovered and no one was convicted.

It took place at the Victoria Club in Queen Street. When Raymond Patrick Bennett – or Raymond Chuck, as he was known – the brilliant ringleader of the gang that pulled it off, yelled out to everyone to get on the floor and keep their heads down, not everyone did. Ambrose Palmer stuck his head up to have a look-see and a voice said, 'You too, Ambrose.'

The person who had called out to Ambrose Palmer was Tony McNamara, one of the gang members. Ambrose had known him since he was a kid. That moment was to have a few ramifications in the criminal world, something we will get to later on.

So, kamikaze street fighting is how I started out, I suppose; then I moved on to guns. I think it was Johnny Harris who gave me a sawn-off .22 and a couple of shells. It was a beautiful little sawn-off .22 rifle, nine inches long with the bolt.

Johnny Harris was known as Cowboy Johnny. He was born in a brothel, his mother being a prostitute in

Prahran. He used to tell me that when he was ten, he would have to stand in the laneways, keeping an eye out for the police, while his mother worked another customer. She died in a mental hospital sometime in the 1960s. He never had much of a childhood, did Johnny.

I think the happiest time of his life was when he was hanging around with me in the Surrey Road Gang in South Yarra. We used to say to each other that the gang made the Mafia look like poofs.

Johnny's early life turned him into a pretty good street fighter. Every year at the Melbourne Show, he would box in Jimmy Sharman's boxing tent, as Cowboy Johnny. He did all right.

He wasn't so good with his hands when it came to the medical side of things, though. A girlfriend of Horatio Morris's, an old-time crim and one of my early mentors, accidentally – well, according to her, anyway – shot me in the back. She'd had a fair bit to drink and said she was sorry, which didn't alter the fact that there was a bloody bullet in me. Johnny dug the bullet out. It was a good thing that, even at this early stage of my criminal life, I was developing a reputation for being able to withstand pain – a lot of pain.

I once heard that rugby league coach from Sydney, Jack Gibson, say, 'Pain only hurts if you feel it.' That's a pretty clever thing to say, when you think about it. And when you think about it, I reckon I would have done pretty well as a rugby league player, not feeling any pain as I was running into blokes, wrestling them to the ground and belting them. Maybe if I had been born in Sydney instead of Melbourne, I would have ended up as the next Johnny Raper instead of as the first Mark Brandon Chopper Read.

Horatio Morris was a pretty interesting fellow to learn from along the way. It was him who told me not to get to loving someone too much because you might have to kill them one day. These were the handy little hints you needed to pick up if you were going to survive in the Melbourne criminal world and I have always been very grateful to Horatio for the things he taught me.

I guess we made a pretty good combination in my early days. Horatio was a crim from the old school and regarded as being pretty tough. He'd been shot at and survived. As he got older, though, he probably needed a bit of muscle at his side. I guess that's where I came in nice and handy.

He was also a good person to go to the races with. He had this charming way, usually with the ladies, that just opened doors. I wish I had known back in 1972 what I now know about Talbot Lodge and Piping Lane. I was there at Flemington the day Piping Lane won the Melbourne Cup at forty to one. Still, in the company of Horatio Morris, I had a pretty good time, mixing with some of Melbourne's leading socialites and identities. That was what I always liked about the races: everyone, from the high and mighty to standover men, ended up mixing and, in Horatio Morris's case with the ladies, often matching.

I wrote one of my poems about a day at the races – it's not quite Banjo Paterson, perhaps, but still good enough to get a run here.

A GREAT DAY

Kings, Queens, Knockabouts, Crooks,
All in together,
Like a yard full of chooks
The South Yarra ladies
Out for a fling,
Getting dated by the roughnecks,
As they stand in the betting ring,
The fallen and the famous,
The wealthy and the poor,
All betting money,
And counting up their score,
Everyone's relaxed,
No need to watch your back,
She's a bloody great day,
At the Caulfield racing track.

It was also in the company of Horatio Morris that I tasted Veuve Clicquot for the first time. We gatecrashed a party in Kew that was being held at the house of Prue Acton, the fashion designer. From memory, there was a Miss Australia there too, but we won't go there. I learned that from Horatio Morris, too – a gentleman never tells.

Horatio didn't talk to me much about his family but I recently found out something really interesting about him. His grandfather was Sam Morris, a bloke who holds a special place in the history of world sport. Old Sam was the first Tasmanian to play Test cricket – and the first West Indian. Old Sam's parents emigrated from Barbados to Tasmania, where Sam was born. Old Sam's father was from Barbados and his mother was part-Indian, part-African. This might explain Horatio Morris's skin colour. He always looked to me like an American Indian. The Morrises had come to Australia to be part of the gold rush. They went first to Tasmania but then to Daylesford in Victoria.

Sam proved very proficient at cricket and eventually moved to Melbourne, to play club cricket for Richmond, Carlton, University and South Melbourne. It seems he wasn't a bad all-rounder, and got picked to play in a Test match when a whole bunch of top players went on strike. He also had a great reputation as a groundsman.

Poor old Sam Morris began to lose his sight in his forties and apparently helped to set up blind cricket in Australia; that's the game they play with the bell in the ball. Horatio Morris also went blind in the latter stages of his life. It might have happened after he got bashed in the cells while in police custody. Or it might just have been genetic.

I remember that one day towards the end of his life, Horatio Morris walked into a pub and yelled out a bloke's name. At that stage, he couldn't see more than a few metres in front of him. I said to him, 'Horatio, he's at twelve o'clock, then one inch to the right.' So Horatio took out a gun, aimed it straight ahead, moved it one inch to the right and shot this bloke in the chest.

Back in those early days of the Surrey Road Gang, we all had to do a fair bit of our own medical work because if you went to a doctor with a stab wound or a bullet inside you, the doctor would have to report it to the police.

There was one doctor who wouldn't, a bloke by the name of Dr Bertram Wainer. He didn't like the police much. In fact, he was the reason that three of them, a chief inspector, a superintendent and a constable, went to prison. They were running a protection racket for backyard abortionists, abortion being illegal in those days. Dr Wainer blew the lid on them. I had to call on the services of Dr Wainer occasionally, for a few stitches here and there.

Nobody could help Cowboy Johnny Harris, though, when he died, still very much a young man. I remember the great feeling of loss. Because he didn't know his own father, my father kinda became the father Johnny didn't have. Dad would cook meals for him, so he was around at our place a fair bit. I guess he became the brother I didn't have.

When I was first in Pentridge, doing three months for assaulting police, my father got into a street fight. He won, but took a bit of a beating because the other bloke had knuckle dusters – or knuckle busters, as Dad of course called them. Johnny found out who it was who had belted my old man with knuckle dusters, and smashed his jaw and cut him with a broken beer glass.

I know that over the years I probably gave my dad a lot of stress because of the way I was living. He had about twenty death threats against him, as people thought they could get to me through him. Keith Alfred Read always stood up for his son, no matter what slanderous things were said about me (and there were plenty). I will always be grateful for that.

Cowboy Johnny always stood up for me and I was grateful for that too, but in the end, it cost him his life. He died in a street fight, protecting me. I was on the ground, having the dear life kicked out of me, and he came charging to my rescue. I held him in my arms as he died after someone had taken a broken bottle to his neck.

I wrote a poem in honour of Johnny.

THE COWBOY

His friendship I can't forget, I'll remember him till I die,
And sometimes in the dead of night I think of him and
    cry,
He fought his way into my heart, headbutt, fist and
    tooth,
His shadow always with me, a memory from my youth,
No-one's guts were strong, no-one's heart more true,
And no-one loved him more than me and Dave the Jew,
He gave his life that I should live,
And the dogs who killed him we don't forgive,
That's a tale the Jew won't tell
But all of them now rest in Hell,
The man without a name, a father or a mother,
Cowboy Johnny Harris, you're not forgotten, brother.

With another bloke I'll just call Dave the Jew (I've never divulged Dave's true identity and I won't now), I arranged for Johnny to be cremated – our way.

We took him to a place we knew of at the back of a bloke's garage. We laid him on a ten-inch bed of pine board and put ten inches of pine board over the top of him, covered it with kerosene and set fire to it. We knew that everything would burn out because pine board burns so hot. We kept piling on the pine board and, by the morning, when we raked him over, there was nothing left but ashes.

To us, it was a very private, and very deep and meaningful, send-off. If we hadn't done it, he would have ended up in a pauper's grave. Because he was born in a brothel, Johnny's birth was never registered. Neither was his death. As far as the officials are concerned, Johnny Harris never existed. But he did and he was a very good friend to me.

We put Johnny's ashes in the Prahran swimming pool. He had always told me that when he died he wanted his ashes scattered on water, but not on the sea because he didn't want the fishes eating him. So Dave the Jew and I broke into the pool, and left Johnny Harris's ashes there.

I remember Johnny fondly all these years on for many reasons, including for having given me my first gun, the sawn-off .22. I already knew a fair bit from my father about guns. But having a gun of my own . . . that was pretty special. It had a tiny little pistol grip. I used to load the gun up and go around with it, and if I had any trouble with anyone, I would pull it out and shoot them in the leg.

I remember the first time I shot someone in the leg. It was a Polish bloke who had bashed me up in a fight the year before. He didn't dob me in when I shot him. I felt quite good that first time, when I pulled the trigger, especially when he didn't dob me in. I felt like I was invincible.

He looked at me and then looked down in disbelief. 'What you do, Chopper?' he said in his Polish accent.

'I shot you in the leg,' I said.

'Why you do that, Chopper?' he said.

'Because you beat me up last year,' I answered.

I told him not to say anything to the police and he said, 'No, of course not.'

I said, 'You go now,' and he hobbled off.

I've never seen him since. I know his name but don't want to say it here.

After that, there were a couple more little shootings around the area. I used to hang around the Collingwood and Prahran Housing Commission flats and get involved in trouble there. I would go down with my sawn-off .22, and Johnny and I would take sides, always with the underdogs. We never knew why they were fighting. We would just poke our heads in and say, 'Do you need a hand?' I shot a couple of people in the leg, around the groin region, in the hip and the back of the leg.

I used to cut the ends of the bullets and make a cross to turn them into dumdums, to make them twice as powerful when they hit someone. You can get .22 hollow points, but it was better to split the bullets open with a knife and fire them that way, so that they expanded on impact.

Dumdums were apparently originally designed for shooting animals with thick skins. They worked on a few thin-skinned types of my acquaintance as well. And they were named dumdums not because of the people who got in the way of them but after a place in India, near Calcutta, where the British first started experimenting with them in the nineteenth century.

Terry the Tank was another member of the Surrey Road Gang. He's a pillar of society these days, so I won't give his full name.

Terry the Tank was bigger than me, which, at that time, was saying something. It was he who sabotaged my nineteenth birthday party. Because Seventh Day Adventists don't like parties, I didn't really have any when I was growing up. So, when I turned nineteen, I thought I would make up for this in one go. I invited just about everyone I knew and told them to bring as many friendly girls as they could. There were people from a whole range of criminal elements invited, except I didn't tell anyone apart from Terry who else I had asked.

Trouble was, Terry the Tank did tell, so there I was, sitting in my little one-bedroom unit with a bathtub full of grog and ice, and nobody turned up except for my father and a couple of others. Terry had frightened everyone else off by telling them that all these members of other gangs were going to be there. They all thought it was going to be one big bloodbath, as distinct from a bloody bath full of grog. So I had to wait until I turned fifty to have my first real birthday party. And I bloody well didn't invite Terry the Tank.

I met Mad Charlie when I was seventeen and a half, and he was fifteen and a half. He was Hungarian and looked thirty-five. He had a bald head, broken nose and cauliflower ears. He looked like a younger version of Marlon Brando in *The Godfather*.

He just idolised people in the crime world and read all the books on the Mafia and knew all its history. As I once wrote about him, 'Charlie studied Mafia crime books like a priest studied the Bible.'

When his family emigrated to Australia, he said to his mother, 'Where is the Statue of Liberty?' He thought he was going to America, not Australia. He really wanted to try his luck in New York and I reckon he would have done quite well there.

When he spoke, he even sounded like Marlon Brando in *The Godfather*. He'd say, 'Hey, Chopper, how you go?'

Everyone was calling me Chopper by then. They had been for a long time. It had all started back in Grade Two, with my old man. He got the name from the Hanna-Barbera Yakky Doodle cartoon. Yakky Doodle was a talking duck who lived with his best friend, Chopper the bulldog. Yakky was always getting into danger courtesy of Fibber Fox or Alfy Gator. Chopper defended him all the time, bashing up Fibber Fox and Alfy Gator. He'd say to Yakky Doodle, 'Put your little wings over your eyes,' and go and do something to the fox and leave him dazed, and Yakky would fly safely back up into his tree house. My old man called me Chopper till the day he died. I would rather be called Chopper than late for lunch. I know people who would prefer to call me Chopper rather than Mark. Sometimes when people get introduced to me, they go to say 'Chopper' but end up saying 'Mark'. It is like someone when meeting an

Aboriginal person saying 'Aborigine' instead of 'Abo', which is what they might really like to say.

Anyway, Mad Charlie, he was a whole different kettle of fish. He was an out-and-out crook and had this idea of robbing massage parlours, because they were also run by crooks and so they couldn't dob you in to the police.

He had a little gang: Mad Archie; Garry the Greek (Garry Calloupes was his real name); and me . . . Chopper Read. We used to run around town knocking off massage parlours, in a cherry-red GT-HO that belonged to Mad Archie. It had automatic transmission and we would scream up to the front of the massage parlours. We'd all jump out and rush around like wild Indians, and I would have a baseball bat ready to go. Then we'd realise Charlie wasn't with us, and we'd look back and he would be sitting in the back seat of the car.

So I would turn back and he would say, 'That's right, Chopper, always remember the Don!' I would open the door for him and he would finally get out.

Mad Archie would then pick a fight, and be punching and fighting like a thrashing machine. Charlie would be talking to the manageress of the massage parlour, who would be saying, 'I don't have any money.'

He would bash her, she would burst into tears and give him the cash box, and there would be $3000 or so in it. Charlie would get the sheila to give him the money first, when I was still out in the hallway, or else-where engaged on the premises, with the baseball bat. He would take $2000 and put it in his pocket and then give $1000 back to her. When I walked in, he would get her to give him the $1000 and then give me $500 and say, 'Look at this, Chopper, we are even.' It was the armed robbery squad that told me he was ripping me off like this.

I didn't do anything to him, though; I couldn't hurt the bugger and I couldn't give a rat's arse about money. It was just about having a bit of fun with Charlie for me. There was always enough money to live on and I really adored Charlie. I did right up to the time he died. As I mentioned, the night before my son Charlie was born, I got a phone call out of the blue from Mad Charlie. I was on the farm down in Tasmania and he wouldn't give me a number to phone him back on. But he said that if I ever came back to Melbourne, he would hear about it and come and visit me.

'In friendship or in anger?' I asked.

'In friendship, of course,' he replied.

I just hope he meant that, because it was the last time I spoke to him. He was killed in 1999 – shot dead outside his own house, part of the long string of gangland killings in Melbourne.

When Charlie and the rest of our gang were running around knocking off massage parlours, I was living in a boarding house with my father at 1 Hawksburn Road, South Yarra. The other day, I came across a list of notable people who lived in South Yarra at some stage in their lives. It included Alfred Deakin, the prime minister; Sir Norman Brookes, the tennis player; and Sir Keith Murdoch, Rupert's dad. And, bugger me; the list also contained one of my first sworn mortal enemies, Dennis

Allen; the bloke whose skull I egg-shelled in Pentridge. He was a drug dealer, and they put him on this bloody list of notable people who've lived in South Yarra, but there was no mention of Chopper Read.

Back when Dad and I, and Dennis bloody Allen, were living in South Yarra, it wasn't the posh sort of place it is now, with lots of boutiques and fancy restaurants. It could be pretty dangerous; especially on one night in 1977, when I was out going for a bit of a walk to the shops.

I had just got out of jail. I was about twenty-three then and there I was, walking along Rockley Road, when I saw this bloke get out of his car and start to look at a map on the bonnet. He had a torch in one hand and was holding the map on the bonnet with the other. He was putting on a very good show of being lost and when he asked me where a certain street – Cromwell Road, it was – might be, I decided to put on a good show of being a good Samaritan. That was my first mistake.

I bent over to look at the map to show him where the street was. He had a gun under it. By the time I saw it in the light of the torch, it was too late.

The next thing I knew, I've got a set of handcuffs on and am in the boot of his car – a Monaro, from memory.

I knew who this person was but have never named him. I won't now, except to say he was from the Painters and Dockers, and, no, not the rock band, the union.

In fact, he had the most awful taste in music. Dean Martin was playing in his cassette player. So, there I am in the boot of this Monaro, being driven God knows where, listening to Dean Martin singing his greatest hits.

As well as the music, I remember other things like it was yesterday, like the smell of the petrol and the sound the tyres made as they went over the tram tracks. I can remember thinking that I wasn't going to give up without a fight.

But if I tried to kick my way out of the boot, he would just turn around and shoot me through the back seats. Monaros don't have bullet-proof back seats.

But this bloke, I concluded, had made his first mistake too. He should have shot and killed me when he first had the chance, when he took me by surprise with the map trick.

We ended up in a spot that looked like bushland. He had found that, all right, without the need of any bloody map. He knew exactly where he was going – out in the cold and lonely bush, for his own version of the famous Frederick McCubbin painting *A Bush Burial*. Except there were to be no grieving onlookers and a dog. That's if you didn't count this dog.

Anyway, he stopped the car and came around and opened the boot, and told me to get out. Getting out of a boot while handcuffed is not easy, and I was a bit off balance when I suddenly realised this was going to be a bit more than a killing. It was going to be a bashing and a killing.

He hit my head with the butt of the pistol and started kicking me. As I put my hands up to defend myself, I thought, 'He's made a second mistake here – he's handcuffed my hands in front of me.'

But that was because he had a job for me . . . digging my own grave. He gave me a garden spade and told me to start digging.

All the time I was digging, I was shitting myself that I was going to die. Literally, I shat my pants. That is the only time in my adult life I've lost control of my bowels. But I still had to keep on digging this hole, my grave.

Then I got him to make another mistake. I told him it would be a lot easier for me to dig my own grave if I didn't have handcuffs on.

He took them off me and I got on with the digging. I was trying not to let him know I was shit-scared, literally. I just got on with digging the hole, my mind racing, thinking what I could do to get myself out of this situation.

I was laughing and joking with him, and he said, 'You're a tough bastard, Chopper, I'll give you that.'

He didn't know it then, but they were going to be the last words he ever spoke. Well, that and the word 'no', which we will get to in a minute.

I was digging away like, well, a bloody gravedigger, and this hole was getting deeper and deeper, and I knew that pretty soon it was going to be deep enough.

So I had to do something pretty quickly. I made out I had hit a hard bit of ground with the spade and shifted my hand to get a better grip on the handle. But instead of hitting the ground, I swung around and hit him in the left kneecap.

Another calculation I had made was that, yes, he had the gun, but a bloke with a smashed kneecap isn't going to be able to shoot too straight. I just had to make sure I hit him real hard. I reckon I nearly cut off his leg with that first whack.

I leaped out of the grave and that's when he spoke the last word he ever spoke while living on Mother Earth: 'Nooooooooo!'

I landed the spade in his brain.

He was dead before he hit the ground, I reckon.

Then I chopped him up with the garden spade before I put him in the grave that he had had me digging for myself. I took his gun off him, and his gold rings, and his car keys, because I needed those to drive myself home. The reason I cut his body up is that if you don't do that, gases will build up in a body and, as they dissipate, cause it to rise by as much as three feet. And if that happened, someone might discover the grave.

I filled in the grave, and drove his car over it time and time again, to flatten it. Then I got out of the car and put a log on top of the grave, still doing everything I could to try to hide it.

At one stage, I thought I heard someone walking through the bushes. In the state of mind I was in, I reckon I would have killed that person too. But the noise went away.

Anyway, after I had finished with my gravedigging duties, I jumped into his car and drove off. It wasn't until I found a road sign that I realised he had driven me to Mount Donna Buang, eighty kilometres from the centre of Melbourne. It's also the closest ski field to Melbourne, not that I needed to know that at the time. I thought that it had certainly all gone downhill for this bloke after he made the fatal mistake of taking the handcuffs off me.

I went back once to try to find what had been supposed to be my final resting place but never could.

Anyhow, I went home and when I woke up the next morning, I wasn't sure at first if I'd dreamed the whole business. Then I looked in the mirror and saw the bruises from when he had bashed my face with the gun. It was true, all right.

Funny thing was, no one ever seemed to miss this bloke. Or, if they did, I never got to hear about it.

All up, it was a character-building exercise, a lesson in life and almost death. I learned a few things that night – like never go to the shops without your guns. And when you kill someone and bury them, it's always a good idea to chop them up, and to put some water and fertiliser in there as well. Because you never know what might grow.

That night was probably the inspiration for the song in *Chopper the Musical* 'Every Day Above Ground Is a Good Day'.

Speaking of songs with inspirational themes, back in 1977 the Bee Gees were wandering around in their tight pants, singing 'Ah, ha ha ha, staying alive'. For me, it was about wandering around just doing my best to stay alive.

One night down in Port Melbourne, two blokes with baseball bats nearly pummelled me to death. In fact, they thought I *was* dead, which is why they stopped hitting me. Funny thing is, I have outlived the both of them. Ha ha.

As I was getting more and more into the world of crime, my father knew what I was doing but didn't mind as long as I wasn't hurting any ordinary people; as long as I confined everything to the criminal world, he was okay. He used to say, 'As long as you don't hurt women, children or old people, Chopper.'

That was why I was so dirty on the Walsh Street murders. That was the killing of two policemen in 1988, apparently because the police had just killed Graeme Jensen, another crim of my acquaintance and one of my enemies from Pentridge.

He had an interesting career, including holding some sort of record for being one of the youngest-ever armed robbers in the history of Victoria. When he was fifteen, he stole around $1400 from the National Bank in Fitzroy.

Jensen was shot dead by members of the armed robbery squad, at a shopping centre in Narre Warren in 1988. The squad was trying to arrest him for a robbery in Brunswick, in which a security guard had been killed. Jensen hadn't been part of that robbery, but the squad thought he was. They staked out his house, and when he came outside to go down the street to get a spark plug for his lawnmower, they chased him. They pulled him over, but he tried to get away by whacking the car into reverse. One of the coppers yelled out that he had a gun and the next thing you know, Graeme Jensen was dead.

At the time, Jensen's allies were pissed off at the way he was killed. There was a belief that the coppers had a plan to take a number of armed robbers out of the system.

The next day, these two young coppers – Steven Tynan, aged twenty-two, and Damian Eyre, aged twenty – were lured into a trap in Walsh Street and shot.

This was supposed to be revenge for the killing of Jensen.

It wasn't revenge, something I believe to be noble, it was just cowardice. These two young coppers hadn't killed Graeme Jensen. It was the armed robbery squad that had killed him.

If these people wanted revenge, why didn't they just walk into the armed robbery squad office and open up on them? That would have been real revenge. They could have shot ten to twelve members of the squad.

Victor Peirce, Trevor Pettingill, Anthony Farrell and Peter McEvoy were charged with the Walsh Street murders. They were acquitted.

The eight police involved in the death of Graeme Jensen were all charged with murder. Seven got the charges made against them withdrawn. In 1995, seven years later, it took the jury just eighteen minutes to find the copper who pulled the trigger not guilty.

Whatever the real story is about the death of Graeme Jensen, the real question is, why kill two innocents?

In my experience, crims never shoot at police when there is a chance of being shot back at. They always shoot in an ambush situation.

The underworld is a strange place, with all sorts of strange rules that some people uphold and some don't. My old man told me never to touch innocents and I never have. Charlie might have hit a few women, the ones who managed the massage parlours, but basically we kept to those rules.

We were stealing the profits of drug dealing, prostitution and gambling. The drugs were marijuana and some powders. I didn't know what they were then, but Charlie knew. I eventually worked out they were heroin.

As I said, we did quite a few hits on massage parlours. We'd do a few in one area, then move on to a new one. There were plenty around. You'd rob a few in St Kilda, so you'd then go to Glenferrie or Caulfield, or St Kilda East or Elwood. We did the Crest Massage Parlour in Armadale. Charlie chose that one.

It was just a case of robbing these people who had money they shouldn't have had, because they were selling heroin and heroin kills people. These drug dealers were driving around in their Mercedes convertibles like they owned the world. So we thought we'd take some of their money off them.

IN 1973, when I was eighteen or so, I met the bloke I've always called Dave the Jew. And I met another big old guy, from Northern Ireland. He had been a heavyweight boxer in America and looked like it: nearly a hundred kilos, a broken nose, head like John Wayne's, with big cauliflower ears, big hands, broken knuckles, and he spoke in a Belfast accent.

Dave the Jew was a bit of a gunman but one without a criminal record. Even now, when he's not half the man he used to be, I won't reveal his full identity.

Dave the Jew said he knew a bloke who worked on a ship; that he would come off this ship and bring in about two pounds of pure heroin. While in Melbourne, he would exchange the heroin for cash.

Dave the Jew said, 'I know what house he is staying in and I know where he does the exchange.' So he hid under this house with a sleeping bag, half a dozen tins of baked beans, a big bottle of water and a double-barrelled shotgun. He was under there for two bloody days. I thought to myself, 'What sort of madman hides under someone's house for two days?' The answer is, Dave the Jew!

I used to walk up to the house and say, 'You all right, Dave?' and he would call out, 'Go away, go away, Chopper; you'll give me up.' So I'd go away, still thinking that Dave the Jew was completely mad.

Anyway, this bloke off the ship eventually staggered up his driveway after the second night. Dave the Jew went into the house and by the time the Irishman and I got there, he had the poor bugger handcuffed.

We put him in the back of the car and drove to a pub in Port Melbourne. Dave the Jew knew the owners and they let us use the keg cellar. We took this bloke down there, sat him on a chair and Dave said, 'Get his shoes off.' We had a hand-held gas bottle with a burner on the top of it.

I said, 'Where is the money, where are the drugs; do you have any?'

He said, 'No.'

I said to Dave, 'Did he come home with anything? Did he have anything in his hands?'

Dave said, 'I didn't notice him carrying anything, I can't remember. I was too busy trying to get the handcuffs on him.'

'Just burn him and find out where it is.'

Dave took this bloke's shoes off and put the blow-torch on his feet. They started to burn and there was a horrible stink, a bit like burned pork and burning hair.

The next thing, the door opened and there was the publican's wife standing there. And, of course, she started to scream.

Dave looked up from his blowtorch handiwork and said, 'Do something!'

So the Irishman knocked the publican's wife out. Then the publican, who had heard his wife's scream, came in and saw her lying unconscious. He didn't want to interfere too much, so he picked her up and dragged her up the stairs.

By then, it was pretty much time for us to leave. So Dave put a fire extinguisher on this bloke's burning feet. Then we put him in the back of the car and drove him back to Webb Dock in Port Melbourne.

The Irishman helped put him on board his ship because, with his burned feet and everything else, he was pretty out of it. He would have woken up the next morning on his boat, wondering what had happened to him, and probably why it had happened to him. And it was all a bloody waste of time.

That sleeping bag is probably still under the house, if the house is still there. None of us were going back to get it.

We had to pay the publican a few bob for his time and trouble in letting us use the keg cellar, and probably for knocking out his wife, and the whole thing was a fucking nightmare. All this because Dave the Jew said this bloke had money.

To this day, I don't know if he was a drug dealer, or had any money. Dave the Jew turned out to be a bit unreliable with his information.

One time, Dave said we had a contract to go and shoot that Catholic bloke who used to be on the television, Bob Santamaria. He's the bloke who split the Labor Party and set up the Democratic Labor Party, a pretty right-wing sort of organisation. They hated the way the communists had, apparently, taken over the unions and the Labor Party.

Dave had an address where he said we had to shoot Bob fucken Santamaria. So off we went. And there we were, sitting outside the house, and the Irishman began singing that Lionel Rose song 'Let Me Thank You for Just Being You'.

On 27 February 1968, Lionel Rose had become the first Australian Aborigine to become a world boxing champion, when he outpointed Fighting Harada over fifteen rounds in a fight up in Tokyo. That was for the world bantamweight title. Funny, isn't it; you get a world title for being able to hit, then you get a hit record. That Johnny Young bloke, from *Young Talent Time*, wrote the song for Lionel. I'm not sure that Lionel Rose could sing all that well but it became a hit.

And there was the Irishman, singing it as we sat in the car outside what was supposed to be Bob Santamaria's house.

Dave the Jew said, 'Will you shut up, you out-of-tune, stone-deaf Irishman?'

The Irishman said, 'You call me that again, I will give you a hiding, you Jewish psychopath!'

We've got more guns than God in the car, we're supposed to be getting ready to knock off Bob fucken Santamaria, and they are having an argument about who can sing the best.

In the end, no one got shot.

Bob Santamaria did eventually die, but not until 25 February 1998. He had a big funeral and all that, but it wasn't us who sent him to his grave.

So, why were we sitting there that night, singing and arguing?

Apparently, it all came about because someone had said something to Dave the Jew about killing Bob Santamaria. As I said, Santamaria was a bit of a right-winger and he'd upset a lot of people with his anti-communist propaganda. Dave the Jew used to go to all these left-wing meetings and knock around with communists. He was always going to some fucking meeting to hear someone talk about communism.

Didn't do him any good, poor bugger. He is a schizo now and just wanders the streets. He'd be fifty-six and he looks about sixty-six, with a grey beard.

I wrote a poem for him back in 1991.

THE JEW

He wants no glory, he wants no fame,
Very few men have heard his name,
But as a hunter, he's the best I know,
Non-stop dash, non-stop go,
He sets to work, without a care,
The smell of burning flesh in the air,
He loves to hunt the big deal prankster,
The nightclub flashy gangster,
He plants them in the ground,
Never to be seen,
Safe and sound,
And before they die, they sometimes ask,
Please tell me who are you,
And with a toothless grin, he looks down and says,
Just call me Dave the Jew.

Looking back, I guess that a few times we did use the gas bottle with a bit more success than that night in Port Melbourne. We once got about $30,000.

Another time, we had to shoot some bloke dead and we hid him in the fridge of the Builders Arms Hotel. We then cut him up and buried the pieces under the Westgate Bridge.

It was Dave the Jew who shot him the first time, and then we broke every bone in his body and set fire to his feet. In the end, I shot him to put him out of his misery. He was begging me to shoot him, so I obliged.

I don't think he was ever missed. He was just some drug dealer. As I said before, they were the ones with all the money, money they didn't deserve, as they were killing innocent people with heroin.

I never thought much more about it after we'd bashed 'em, set fire to their feet, or whatever, and got their money. I don't believe I ever had a thought like 'This is not the way to live my life.' I thought it was the way to live. I thought life was good. That's the way it is.

There's another Dave the Jew story I should probably tell you. It features another Irishman, by the name of Dion. He was a seaman too, and used to come to Melbourne about once a year. On one of his annual visits to Melbourne, in 1977, he and Dave the Jew got into a blue.

Dave the Jew rang me up and said, 'Can you come around to my place, Chopper?'

He had a place in South Yarra. I went around there and there was Dion, with almost as many holes in him as a Swiss cheese. Dave the Jew had got all excited and shot him in the chest, the buttock and the leg.

Dion could not be taken to hospital or Dave the Jew's spotless criminal record would have been tainted. And, even worse, unless he got this bloke out of there and the place cleaned up, Dave the Jew's mum and dad would have found out what he had done.

So we took Dion to another bloke's house, where we proceeded to operate on him to get the bullets out. We gave him a hit of heroin to knock him out. Just to make sure he was out of it, I knocked him out twice. While he was out, we used a razor blade to cut out the bullets. We gave him a bottle of antibiotics, bandaged him up, and Dave the Jew nursed him for the next ten days.

He survived and, last I heard of him, he was in South Africa.

I still laugh when I think about it.

I've got this far and haven't talked about one of the things for which I am allegedly famous in addition to burning people's feet – toecutting. This is part of the high-risk, high-reward business of robbing from other criminals, mostly drug dealers. Sometimes you'd turn up with a set of bolt cutters and ask them to remove their shoes. Sometimes you didn't even have to ask them to remove their shoes . . . you just asked them what their shoe size was. It was pretty clear you were thinking of reducing that shoe size a bit.

These people caused me to have a pretty poor opinion of a lot of crims. They would shit themselves and hand over the money.

Drugs have ruined the criminal world, which once used to be all about gambling and prostitution. All right, you might get a dose of something you weren't expecting from a prostitute. And you might lose a few bob gambling. But drugs kill people. And the people who sold drugs knew that, but still kept on selling them because they were greedy. Greed and drugs have been a big problem in the Melbourne underworld. That was the combination that produced all the stuff you see on *Underbelly*.

I could always make a pretty good living as a toe-cutter, or a head-hunter, which was another bit of criminal slang for living off the profits of other crims.

In 1987, when I was out of Pentridge after doing time for kidnapping a county court judge, I had a lot of people paying me money just so I was on their side. There were people running illegal card games, and running massage parlours. They'd be giving me $200, or some other amount, a week.

Even when I went to Tasmania after doing four years for shooting Chris Liapis and burning down Nick the Greek's house, there were people who were happy to pay me to stay away from Melbourne.

As a young toecutter, I quickly learned there was a real art to getting money out of drug dealers. You'd burst in on them and the first thing they'd do would be to try to hide the drugs. I wasn't interested in the drugs, never was. All I wanted was the money. They'd have trouble remembering where the money was. So I had a brainwave. I would threaten to burn their drugs, or flush them down the toilet.

Shit, that worked every time. These dealers were so in love with their drugs, you only had to pick up a bag of pills or powder and walk towards the toilet, and they immediately wanted to start giving you money.

I had no need of the drugs. If I stole the drugs, the only way to get any money was to sell them, and I've already told you what I think of drug dealers and their calling in life. It is a limp-wristed way to make a living in the criminal world. But being a toecutter, a foot burner, a head-hunter, robbing from other crims who, of course, couldn't dob you in to the coppers, that was pretty smart.

It is my opinion that the Melbourne crime scene pretty much began to change for the worse after the

1976 Great Bookie Robbery. To me, that was a good old-fashioned crime, brilliantly conceived by Raymond Bennett. In fact, he had made a trip back from England to check if it was feasible. He was out on parole from a prison there, where he had ended up while part of the famous Kangaroo Gang.

This gang, which also included Pat 'Fibber' Warren, robbed jewellers and fashion houses in England and Europe. They were as game as anything, doing these robberies in broad daylight. Good-looking women were involved too. They were sent into the shops to keep the staff occupied.

Raymond Bennett had to go back to England to finish his sentence but, as he flew out, was pretty confident he could pull the robbery off. What used to happen was that the Melbourne bookies would all meet at the Victoria Club to settle their debts. Armoured trucks carrying huge amounts of money would roll in. It had been done this way for years and nobody thought a lot about it. There was no real security, except for a few members of the consorting squad, who also used to hang out around the Victoria Club. Interestingly, they were nowhere to be seen on this day.

Raymond Bennett had about half a dozen blokes all trained up to do the Great Bookie Robbery. They stormed into the Victoria Club and told everyone to hit the decks, and started helping themselves to somewhere between $1.2 million and $12 million, all stuffed into three duffel bags. The amount is in dispute because, you see, the bookies never did, ahem, want to say just how much they had won or lost.

Only one person was ever charged – Norman Lee. He was a professional money launderer and dim sim manufacturer. Now, that's a CV to be proud of. Some of the money might have gone into buying him new equipment with which to make dim sims. Whatever, the moneys were dispersed very quickly.

There is a story that, shortly after the robbery, Raymond Bennett's mother collapsed while visiting her solicitor. When the ambos undid her clothing to begin treating her, they found she had $90,000 worth of cash on her. She had obviously planned on getting a few groceries on the way home from the solicitors.

Even though they got away with it, it wasn't at all a fairytale-happy ending. Raymond Bennett was shot and killed in November 1979. It happened in the hallway that led from the holding cells at the Melbourne Magistrates Court.

Everyone went ballistic when the shots were fired and, in all the confusion, the killer got away. Some people suggest it was Brian Kane, doing it as revenge for the killing of his brother, Leslie Kane; not that Brian Kane necessarily pulled the trigger, though some think he did. More likely, with a bit of help from people in high places, he arranged for someone else to pull the trigger – Christopher Dale Flannery. Now, there is a name that kept reappearing in both Melbourne and Sydney for years, usually shortly after someone had been killed or disappeared.

There are all sorts of stories about him, his deeds, and his nickname – Mr Rentakill. The story I like the most is the one in which the screws at Pentridge told

Flannery they were moving him into a cell next to mine, and he shat himself and barricaded himself into his old cell. Christopher Dale Flannery also got his lawyers to take action under some Human Rights Act to keep him in his old cell.

It turned out the screws were only teasing. Ha ha.

Anthony Paul McNamara, the bloke who had been identified by Ambrose Palmer during the Great Bookie Robbery, died of a drug overdose. He knew from the moment Palmer heard his voice that the game was pretty much up for him. However, he didn't tell the other members of the gang, especially Raymond Bennett, that he knew Palmer had recognised him. If he had, Ambrose Palmer would have died that day.

Still, word got out, probably because Palmer told one person confidentially, who told another person confidentially and, soon enough, people knew who had done it.

And that's when the Kane Brothers got involved. They wanted a share of the profits, something they were used to getting in those days. They were tough standover merchants.

Raymond Bennett said no to the Kanes and probably had Les Kane killed, just to let him know he meant it. I really admired Raymond Bennett for his toughness and clever planning.

He could also be kind. When I was stabbed five times by Jimmy Loughnan, it was Raymond Bennett who came and reassured me about my future. I respected him a lot for that.

I didn't think too highly of him, though, regarding his claim that he punched and defeated one of the famous Kray brothers, Reggie, while he was in prison in England and lived to tell the story. From my understanding of things over there, if you belted a Kray brother, the whole of English villainy descended on you.

The story I heard was that there was an altercation with Reggie Kray, but Raymond Bennett came off second best. And when he got out of prison, he was driven to Heathrow, after a good beating, and told never to come back.

Norman Lee was killed by police in 1992, while, allegedly, attempting to rob an armoured van.

Although I did a lot of armed robberies too – none anywhere near as big as the Great Bookie Robbery – I was only ever found guilty of that particular offence once.

The cops had all of us, Mad Charlie and the rest, on about thirty charges but said that if we pleaded guilty to one, they would drop the other twenty-nine.

I said all right.

THE FIRST time I was arrested was when we were trying to rip the door off a nightclub storeroom but the owner was still inside.

I was trying to help out a little Yugoslav bloke I knew, who just wanted to break into somewhere and see what he could get. I told him I knew this club where we could rip the door off and see what was inside. Well, the owner was inside.

He rang the police, and they came around and caught us. I calmly went with them. No fuss, no bother. That was because I respected the police, who were only doing their job. I was sent to Turana Boys Home for three months.

The second time I got arrested, I did three months for bashing three bouncers. It turned out they were off-duty police officers and they wanted to arrest me for assaulting police.

I said, 'That's not fair, you're bouncers. You can't have two jobs.'

They said, 'Oh yes, we can,' and so I went with them after that, and got three months for assaulting police. I served those three months in Pentridge, even though I was only seventeen. I've always thought you weren't supposed to go to Pentridge until you were eighteen. I never worked out why that didn't apply to me in this case. I just know I ended up in Pentridge. These days, my brother-in-law, Ron, reckons that there was some rule that allowed them to put people who were under eighteen in Pentridge. In fact, Ron says, the youngest person to go there was fifteen.

Poor bastard.

For those who might not know, Pentridge is a bloody huge jail in Melbourne. Or, it used to be – they closed it down in 1997, when the Victorian Government decided to privatise the prisons.

It's just occurred to me that I should have put in a tender to run one of these private prisons. After all, I've had a fair bit of experience of running prisons.

They're turning Pentridge into a residential area, with a housing estate and shops. I wouldn't want to live there. Apparently, a few others wouldn't either. One of the developers is trying to get rid of as many references to it having been a prison as possible.

Apparently, it turns some people off that they might be living where Chopper Read once slept. Certainly, when you read the fancy words on the brochures about Pentridge Village, you'd never believe it was the same place where I spent a lot of my days: 'Pentridge Village is fast becoming one of Melbourne's residential hotspots as inner-urban living becomes highly desirable.'

They talk about me living off the proceeds of crime. It's criminal that people get paid to write this stuff.

Pentridge was built in 1850 and officially opened in 1851. When it first opened, the prisoners had to sleep on the floor. The poor buggers ate out in the open, rain, hail or shine. The prison officers made them work on the roads in chain gangs. If they tried to escape, the officers put heavier chains on their legs.

Even though he was hanged at the old Melbourne Gaol, Ned Kelly's remains ended up in Pentridge. That's because when they were doing the excavations to build the Royal Melbourne Institute of Technology, they disturbed Ned's original grave. Such is life, and death, I suppose.

A lot of blokes who got hanged were also buried at Pentridge, but they've dug up most of their bodies too since they closed it down. They were all buried behind D Division. There were no headstones, just little markers made out of oak. Some of the bodies have been given to the men's families. Others are in the morgue.

All up, eleven people got hanged at Pentridge, the last one being Ronald Ryan, on 3 February 1967. I don't remember a real lot about that, other than that it happened. I was around thirteen at the time.

Some pretty famous names have been visitors of Her Majesty at Pentridge over the years, some of whom you mightn't automatically think of: Derryn Hinch, the broadcaster; John Nicholls, the footballer from Carlton. And Mark Read, the author.

Pentridge has had a few nicknames – the Bluestone College and the College of Knowledge. And the Bash House. It has probably always had a reputation for being ferocious in the way prisoners were treated.

I certainly treated a few prisoners ferociously when I was in there. And a few prisoners treated me pretty ferociously too. I've got the scars to prove it, all over my body. Stab wounds, Stanley knife wounds, razor blade wounds.

It was a place where you had to be more merciless than everyone else, 'cause there was never a lot of mercy around.

I remember that the third time I went to prison, Little Peter Allen came up to me and told me, 'Pull your head in.' This wasn't Peter Allen the poofy bloke who sang 'I Go to Rio'. This was a bloke who was a heroin dealer and, at one stage, was in the top ten of Victoria's most wanted. So, he had a bit of a reputation, even though he wasn't all that tall, and he was just wanting to let me know who was boss.

I had other ideas about who should be boss. I leaned over him and asked, 'Who are you talking to, you little squirt?'

Even though I was still pretty young then, I must have already had a bit of a reputation of my own. Peter Allen became quite nice to me after that. All up, I reckon I've known Peter Allen for about forty years now and, even though I bashed his brother, I'd say we've been on good terms for most of that time.

I remember, with a chuckle, that Peter got the nickname Six Shots pretty early in his criminal career, when he and another bloke, by the name of Allan Rudd, were driving along and a car tried to overtake them.

Peter Allen yelled out to Allan Rudd, 'Six shots rapid fire!'

Allan Rudd responded to the military precision of the order and the nickname stuck.

The first time I went to Pentridge, Mick Woolf and Shane Goodfellow were in there. I had heard of them, and was to hear plenty about them over the years to come; especially about Shane Goodfellow.

They were sharpies from Hawthorn and were involved in a lot of stuff around Melbourne. They were in this time, I think, for assault and robbery. I know they also did a bit of time for belting up a couple of coppers. I think they're both dead now. I know Shane Good-fellow is. He died in 1992, of a drug overdose. The drugs do that to you.

Anyway, there I was in Pentridge for the first time and Mick and Shane were walking up and down, giving everyone dirty looks as we came in.

I said to myself, 'One day I am going to bash that Shane Goodfellow.'

I did.

Years later – in 1979, I believe it was – I met him in the laundry yard, and broke his jaw, collarbone and skull, and then broke his leg as I tossed him out of the window. He hadn't done anything to provoke it. I just did it because I had made that promise to myself.

After I began writing my books, I got a letter from a lady who wanted to know if I had really bashed Shane Goodfellow. I wrote back saying that I had, and she was very grateful to me. She said that Shane Goodfellow and some of his friends had assaulted and raped her.

Bashing before you were bashed was the mindset you had to have if you were going to survive in prison. And over my lifetime, I've had to survive twenty-three and a half years in prison.

The first time was the three months in Turana Boys Home, when I was sixteen and a half. Then it was for assaulting the coppers. That third time, when I got to put Little Peter Allen in his place, I was doing eighteen days for some bloody rubbish. And it *was* just rubbish because I even forget what it was. The next time was three and a half years, for armed robbery of a massage parlour.

Then I did nine and a half years for trying to kidnap a county court judge. The original sentence was for seventeen years with a non-parole period of eleven and a half years.

Then, I got off the charge of murdering Sammy the Turk, but did four and a half years for burning down Nick the Greek's house and shooting Chris Liapis. As I have said many times before, if you knew Nick the Greek you'd want to burn his house down too. I didn't like Liapis much either. He was a drug dealer, a liar and a big-noter, so I shot him.

I later made friends with Chris Liapis; on the radio, of all things. I was part of a talkback radio session on Melbourne's 3RRR. This was on 'The Party Line Show', hosted by Headley Gritter. It goes to air midnight to two am on Sundays and it's been going forever.

Anyway, on this night I was a guest and Chris Liapis rang up. He told me who he was and, much to my shock and surprise, said he didn't have any hard feelings towards me. He said, 'I wish you all the best, Chopper.' I said I felt the same towards him.

So, we parted on friendly terms and I was pretty glad about that. I didn't want to have that old ghost jump up from out of the darkness at me one night and go, 'Hey, Chopper, remember me? Now, here's yours!' BANG BANG. And it could have so easily been like that.

I got out of Pentridge for the last time in 1991, and after that, I went to Tasmania and ended up in the prison at Risdon. There, I did five years and nine months for, of course, shooting the president of the Outlaws Motor Cycle Club, Sidney Michael Collins.

Add it all up and, yep, it's twenty-three years and nine months.

Prison was a dog-eat-dog world.

In Pentridge, I was the number one billet, so I was in charge of handing out the food, cleaning out the cells, cleaning up the shit – all the important jobs. That also included picking up a lot of teeth because a lot of people got bashed.

Speaking of teeth, I had problems with my own while I was in Pentridge, but not because I got bashed. One day, I slipped and fell on a tap and smashed quite a few of my teeth. I got taken to the prison dentist, who was a real master in the art of dispensing pain. He took the broken teeth out of the top of my mouth under anaesthetic, but I don't reckon he bothered with the anaesthetic when he got to the bottom gum.

Ever since, I've had a few lovely sets of false teeth of which I am very proud – platinum teeth, gold teeth and now cobalt teeth. I think that a lot of people, when they see that I have these wonderful sets of false teeth, think I lost the originals getting bashed. But no, it was an accident when I fell onto that tap.

I don't think I had to pick up too many teeth after I bashed Brian Kane, but the story of how I got to whack him is one of my all-time favourites.

He was getting out in a month, so I was running out of time. But, just before he was released, he came to H Division for eighteen days.

I thought to myself, 'How am I going to get this bloke?'

I came up with a grand plan to get him somewhere I could bash him. I have always liked to have grand plans. Margaret calls it me making the big statement.

I mixed human poo with ten litres of hot stew, and added a full packet of Keen's curry powder. I gave it to Kevin Taylor to taste. Taylor was the bloke who shot Pat Shannon during Melbourne's dockies war and was one of four men arrested for the murder.

On 17 October 1973, Shannon was gunned down in the Druids Hotel in South Melbourne. He was having a celebratory drink when a bloke walked in carrying a .22 calibre rifle and shot him three times. Pat Shannon wasn't the only bloke to get killed in the dockies war. They reckon the death toll was somewhere between thirty and sixty. It was a real power struggle for control of the Painters and Dockers Union – or the Federated Ship Painters and Dockers Union, to give them their proper name. In my view, it was a case of some of the old blokes who had been running the Painters and Dockers Union not knowing when it was time to move on and so the young blokes started killing them.

In the end, there was a huge Royal Commission into the whole sorry business, which cost the taxpayer $4 million. In 1984, Frank Costigan QC, the bloke who headed the Royal Commission, said about the Painters and Dockers Union in one of his reports:

The Painters and Dockers Union has attracted to its ranks large numbers of men who have been convicted of, and who continue to commit, serious crimes. They treat the law with contempt, and are scornful of its punishments. They treat law enforcement agencies as their enemies. They are motivated by greed and are not controlled by any consideration for their victims. Violence is the means by which they control the members of the group. They don't hesitate to kill . . .

Pat Shannon's death came after a vote to elect a new head of the Painters and Dockers. Pat Cullen, a former union leader, was counting the votes and told my mate Bill 'The Texan' Longley, one of the candidates, that Bill had 'shit it in'. But then, somehow, apparently at the point of a pistol, the votes got counted again, and this time Pat Shannon had won. This all happened about the same time that a few shots were fired at Bill Longley as he was heading back to the union rooms where the ballot was to be declared.

The other people charged with the death of Pat Shannon were Gary Leslie Harding, Alfred Leslie Cannott and, probably not surprisingly, Bill 'The Texan' Longley. They called him 'The Texan' because he got around in a Stetson and carried a gun with him in his belt.

The Crown Prosecutor reckoned Bill Longley paid Kevin Taylor $6000 to kill Shannon. Whatever, Kevin got charged with murder and ended up in H Division, where he got to do a few little jobs for me, including the cutting of my ears.

But that's another story we will get to later.

It's funny how things go, how over time friendships get formed in and out of prison. One of the people who always supported Margaret through the tough times when I was in jail was Bill Longley. He'd ring her up to make sure she was going okay and even take her ballroom dancing.

Over a long period of time, I have come to think very highly of Bill 'The Texan' Longley – so much so, that I even wrote a poem about him.

THE TEXAN

He's the man they love to hate,
Now they have him behind the gate,

Him and his team were dockland perfection,
They fought the Commies and won the election,
The other crew had to pull up their socks,
So they got Fanny to punch the box,
Pat and Putty said what a top plan,
But that's when the shit hit the fan,
The Pom was busy cutting toes,
The jacks sat back picking their nose,
The word was out The Texan had lost,
But nothing is gained without a cost,
A few broken heads and busted legs,
They were going down like bloody tent pegs,
Someone had a sweet connection,
There wasn't much police protection,
But when in doubt just blame The Texan,
Pat felt safe, it was his big day,
He even had a bodyguard,
But Machine Gun Bobby was trying too hard,
The press roared like thunder,
Someone had to go under,
The other team had plenty to hide,
But the Crown Law gave them a nice free ride,
They couldn't beat him any other way,
So they loaded him up and sent him away.

While Bill Longley was in prison, I went out of my way to make sure no one bashed him. In fact, if truth be known, my Overcoat Gang and I kept Bill alive in Pentridge, because there were plenty of blokes on the other side of the Painters and Dockers argument in there as well. It was well known that if you took on Bill 'The Texan' Longley, you would be taking on Chopper Read too.

I had no real beef with the Painters and Dockers per se; it was just that my worst enemies happened to be Painters and Dockers.

Anyway, back to my story of the pooey curry and Brian Kane. Kevin did the taste test with the curry and said he could taste the Keen's curry powder but there was no taste of poo. So I fed it to everyone in the division. I had to give it to everyone, even though it was only Brian Kane I was after. If a few people were told not to eat the stew because I had put poo in it, they would tell other people not to eat it because Chopper had put poo in it and then no one would eat the stew, including Brian Kane, because Chopper had put poo in it. Two days later, everyone came down with gastroenteritis and were shitting themselves all over the jail: in the cells, the yard, everywhere.

I remember seeing Brian Kane waiting to see the doctor and holding on to his guts, and thinking, 'This is my chance.' And I thought that, even though there were a whole lot of people, including Governor Quinn and other important people in the prison, standing around and watching.

Now, the doctor's door was always left open in H Division. I was in the scullery, watching all this, and the door to the scullery was always left open too. The doctor went off to do something – get some medicine, or whatever, for Brian Kane's gastro – so I rushed out of the scullery and bashed Brian Kane with an iron bar when he was on the gurney, waiting to be treated.

The doctor made a statement against me. And all the other people who had seen it, the governor and all the other screws, made statements against me.

But Brian Kane said, 'No, he never hit me!' So, they couldn't take any action against me. In those days, if the victim didn't give you up in a signed statement or refused to identify you as the attacker – well, they couldn't do anything to you.

That is how I got away with so many things in Pentridge . . . the victims wouldn't give me up. I reckon I got away with more than sixty bashings because of this.

Brian Kane was killed inside a hotel in Melbourne's Brunswick in 1982. His murder is one of the oldest unsolved cases in Victoria.

I nearly killed Kane once, but my dear old dad saved his life.

About a month before this particular event, I had seen Brian Kane talking to the police in the Morning Star Hotel. When he turned up in Rockley Road, South Yarra, right next to my dad's place, I was convinced he was there to kill me. So, I grabbed Dad's dear old Bentley shotgun and shoved both barrels into Brian Kane's mouth. Dad rushed out and calmed things down.

It turned out that Brian Kane was in the vicinity to do a favour for a certain bookmaker called Pat, a good mate of Horatio Morris's. Some bloke who lived near us had apparently given Pat's girlfriend a bit of a whack. A good mate of Horatio Morris's is a good mate of Chopper Read's, and once we found all that out from Brian Kane – well, we all went in and gave this bloke a talking to about not touching our friend Pat's girlfriend.

As I've said, there were a lot of instances in Pentridge of people not giving me up. The last bloke I ever hit in prison was Reshad 'Richard' Mladenich, back in 1991. He was known as King Richard and was the loudest man ever to be behind the walls of Pentridge Prison. I never did like loudmouths.

Mladenich stood six foot two inches tall and weighed a good fifteen to seventeen stone, and was as strong as a bull. He was also a heavy heroin user who, under the influence of drugs, would yell at and abuse everyone he didn't like in the prison.

He didn't like me. But he thought the world of my worst enemy, a man who can't be named at the present time.

My enemy used to write down his occupation as painter and docker but he was a lot of other things. He was an abalone fisherman. He was a killer.

In 1976, he shot an off-duty policeman who tried to stop an armed robbery; shot him in the back. The copper got a medal for bravery. You could call my enemy a lot of things, but never brave.

He has since been exposed as a police informer – a dog. When Graeme Jensen got shot and killed by the armed robbery squad, this man made a statement to the effect that Jensen was carrying a gun. According to this statement, the reason Jensen had a gun was that he was scared of him and his supporters; Jensen had started living with my enemy's missus while he was in prison. He later tried to retract the statement.

I don't think that Graeme Jensen should have been having his way with another man's missus. That's wrong when a man is in jail. But, by making that statement, every man and his dog knows that my enemy is a dog.

Back then, though, while I thought he was a dog, King Richard didn't. He was still under his spell. He was also often under the influence of drugs, and one night he was yelling abuse at me and calling me a dog.

I've never dobbed in anyone in my whole life, so I didn't take kindly to being called a dog. So, I thought, 'I am going to have to remove King Richard's crown.'

I almost did, with a garden spade.

The morning after King Richard had been calling me a dog, he didn't remember what he had said the night before, so wasn't thinking I might be looking for him. He was standing out in the yard and talking to my good friend Joe 'The Boss' Ditroia.

Years later, even though he was on parole in South Australia, Joe 'The Boss' Ditroia came to Margaret's and my wedding. He then went back to South Australia, told them he had breached the conditions of his parole by leaving the state without permission, and went to jail. That's true friendship.

This day back in Pentridge, as King Richard was talking to the Boss, I grabbed a spade off one of the screws, who were all out doing some gardening. I turned the spade on its side and sliced it through the air at a gentle, easygoing pace.

It hit King Richard in the crown of his head and took the top off like a spoon takes the top off a hard-boiled egg. You could see his brains as his head opened up.

King Richard staggered, then stumbled forward, and dark blue and red blood came pouring out of the wound. He fell over, then got to his feet and looked like he wanted to fight me. The screws grabbed him and took him away.

Members of the homicide squad were at Pentridge that day, and even though King Richard was still alive, and so, technically, it wasn't murder, they questioned the both of us.

They said to him, 'Who did it, Richard?'

He said, 'I fell over and hit my head on a rock.'

They said to him, 'We know it was Chopper Read who hit you.'

He told them that Chopper Read had had nothing to do with it.

They didn't bother charging me, even though two screws and half a dozen other people made statements against me.

Yes, I bashed more than sixty men behind the walls of Pentridge, and all of them have told the investigating police that Chopper Read had nothing to do with it.

They have since changed the law so that no one can bash a fellow prisoner and get away with it if he refuses to dob them in. But I got away with a lot of bashings all through the 1970s and 1980s. I always thought I had to be physically and psychologically on top of the whole division when I was in H Block.

Another little trick of the trade I had learned because of my role as number one billet.

I used to hand out the soap. One day, I stuck all the soap in a big garbage bin and filled it with hot water. The soap became soft. Then I put a razor blade in each bar and put the soap out in the yard to dry.

One of the screws asked me what I was doing.

I said, 'I am drying the soap, sir.'

One of the chiefs said to the screw, 'What is Read doing?'

When he was told I was drying the soap, he said, 'Well, he's certified insane, let him get on with it.'

When you're certified insane, they give you a wide berth in Pentridge, so you can pretty much get away with murder.

Ha ha!

Anyway, two days later, people were starting to cut their throats, their arms, cutting themselves all over as the soap was being worn down and the razor blades exposed.

Then they had to abolish the hard soap. They had liquid soap, until someone put caustic soda into it. I think they've since gone back to the hard soap.

There was a bloke in there by the name of Piggy Palmer; that's not his real name but that's what I called him.

He would eat two bread rolls in his cell every night at eleven-thirty. He would lather them with butter and put a liberal amount of jam on them. I used to clean out his cell every day, and there would be butter, jam and crumbs on his bed and on his desk.

One day, I went down to the labour yard where they kept the shit buckets and got hold of a fingerful of shit and put it into a clean tin. I then said to the screws that I would go and clean out the cells, and went to Piggy Palmer's cell.

I emptied all the jam out of his tin and then tipped the shit into the bottom. I then put all the jam back on top and carefully patted it down. I checked it to make sure I couldn't smell the shit. I put the lid back on Piggy Palmer's jam, and went back to my cell to wait and see what happened at eleven-thirty, when he discovered the shit in his jam.

The first night I listened and nothing happened. There were still crumbs and butter when I went to clean out his cell the next day, and the jam level had gone down a bit, so I knew he had had his usual late-night snack.

The second night, there was still no sound but the level in the jam tin had gone down to about half and there were crumbs everywhere when I checked things the next day.

Third night, still nothing.

Fourth night and all I could hear were these loud *brrrrrrrrrrrk* noises and the sound of taps running.

The bloke whose name I can't mention yelled out, 'What's going on?'

Charlie Le Fleur, a screw who wore slippers at night, so you couldn't hear him coming, said, 'That's nine days extra.'

He yelled: 'Get fucked!'

Le Fleur said, 'That's another nine days extra!'

A lot of people who came to H Block didn't know that you couldn't make a noise at nighttime. If you did, you got nine extra days, so, if you didn't learn to shut up, two weeks could become three years.

Anyway, the next thing, Piggy Palmer stopped making all these sick *brrrrrrrk* noises and started yelling stuff out. Back then, they wouldn't say my name if I did something because they didn't want to give me up. So, instead of saying 'Chopper did this', or 'Chopper did that', they would yell out 'that bloke' did this, or 'that bloke' did that. So Piggy yelled, 'That bloke, you know that bloke, he's shit in my jam!'

And the whole division cracked up laughing.

Shitting in someone's jam has got to be funny, I don't care what anyone says. And he must have really chowed down on it before he realised there was shit in his jam. I wonder what jam and poo together tastes like!

When I got to H Division, one of the first things the prison officers said to me was 'No talking on the phones, Chopper.'

I didn't know what they meant at first, because you didn't have a phone in your cell, but I soon worked it out. You'd hear tapping on the pipes coming through your toilet. What I did then, and the bloke in the cell next to me would do, and the blokes in the cells above us would do, is empty all the water out of our toilets. Then we'd talk to each other through the pipes. You had to pump the water out with your hand, so we kept the toilets very clean with Ajax and stuff like that, and then we could talk to people for hours.

I guess the screws could listen at the cell door to one conversation, but wouldn't be able to hear what the other person was saying. So, it was a pretty good way of communicating.

I probably should tell you about another bloke in Pentridge for whom I still have a lot of time – a fine specimen of humanity by the name of Frankie Waghorn. I have always been glad that Frankie Waghorn was on my side. He had the best punch you could ever want to see.

That's why I am not convinced he was guilty of the murder of John Turner, who was stabbed to death in 1989. Frankie Waghorn didn't need a knife to kill anyone. He could do it with his fists. As I said, I was always happy to have Frankie on my side when we were in Pentridge together because you needed all the friends you could get.

THE LONGEST stretch I did in prison was for kidnapping a county court judge in January 1978. I did this, or tried to do it, because a fella by the name of Jimmy Loughnan, a real good friend of mine at the time, had written to me asking for help to get him out of prison so he could see his girlfriend.

He was up in J Ward in Ararat Prison in country Victoria. Until 1991, J Ward was a place the criminally insane were kept. Even worse for Jimmy Loughnan, it had a track record of keeping people there forever. Now it's a tourist attraction where they take visitors from all over the world on a guided tour and tell them about all the depraved people who were inmates. They probably tell them about Jimmy Loughnan, Chopper Read's mate.

J Ward was originally built as a jail in 1859, during the gold rush days in Victoria. When the gold rush ended, it was taken over by the Lunacy Department – what a name.

A man called Bill Wallace was in there for sixty-four years, until he died at the age of 108. And he wasn't the record-holder for being there the longest. That record belonged to Charles Fossard – this poor bastard was stuck in J Ward for seventy-one years. So, J Ward was a bit like the Australian cricket team. It was harder to get out of than into.

Luckily for me, I only ever spent two weeks in J Ward. It was around 1978 or 1979, I reckon. After I had had my ears cut off, I was taken to G Division and then had my couple of weeks in J Ward.

It was a terrible place.

People slept on a concrete floor. There was a shit bucket in the middle of the room. Meal times were like feedings of animals. Some of the people couldn't have their straightjackets removed, they were that mad. So the people still wearing their straightjackets would just dunk their heads into the bowls of food.

When I got this letter from Jimmy, asking me to do something to get him out of J Ward, I wrote back saying, 'The best way to get you out is to kidnap a judge and demand you be let out.' I had read somewhere that political activist Angela Davis had done it in America. She was supposed to be behind the attempted kidnapping of not just a judge but a whole jury. Four people, including the judge, ended up dead.

So, it had been attempted in America, if a little unsuccessfully, but had never been done in Australia. I thought Chopper Read could have a crack at being the first. I said to Jimmy, 'If I kidnap a county court judge and they want him back, why wouldn't they release you?'

I went to the fifth court on the fifth floor of the County Court. It was Australia Day. I am not sure why I chose Australia Day to do it; it kinda just happened, I suppose. I just walked up to the fifth floor and five coppers walked in behind me. I went up to the judge, put a sawn-off shotgun in his mouth and said, 'Release my best friend, Jimmy Loughnan.' The judge pushed me back and coppers came from everywhere. They ripped my belt off and used it as a choker, and dragged me down to the cells.

I got seventeen years with an eleven and a half minimum and ended up getting out after nine and a half years.

I later wrote to Judge Martin to apologise for my actions. I told him I had nothing against him, that I was just trying to get Jimmy Loughnan out of J Ward. He wrote back, said he had no hard feelings towards me and wished me all the best for the future. That was a future that included a long time in HM Prison, Pentridge.

I knew that with such a long sentence in front of me, I would have to lay down the rules pretty quickly. At that time, the screws had a bit of a reputation for belting the prisoners as a sort of little welcoming ceremony. Not for nothing was Pentridge also known in some quarters as the Bash House. The belting wasn't going to happen to me.

I hid a razor blade in the roof of my mouth. I walked up to George Burcheck, who was the superintendent of H Block at the time, and took the razor blade from my mouth to show George I had it. He immediately confiscated the razor blade. I then ran my finger down the side of his throat, across his jugular vein.

I said to him, 'The first one of your screws that touches me, George, I will watch and I will wait and I will take that officer's life right here in this division.

After that, you can lock me up in your cells or do what you want. If you take me to court, I will plead guilty. You can even hang me in my cell. But I will kill that officer. So if any of your screws bash me, George, you tell that screw to say goodbye to his family every day when he leaves for work, like he was saying goodbye to them for the last time. Because one day, it will be his last day on earth, because I will cut his jugular and he will be dead before he has the chance to see his family again.' I explained to George, not that he needed me to, that if a person's jugular was severed, they would be dead within eight minutes. 'They would be dead before the ambulance could get here to take them to hospital,' I told him.

After that happened, all the prison officers would come, one by one, to my cell, open the little trap door and say in a bit of a whisper, 'Now, listen, Chopper, we are not going to hurt you. We don't hurt prisoners in H Division. We don't know where you heard that but we don't go bashing prisoners in our system.' Then they all added that none of them were frightened by anything I had said to George Burcheck. But they all came to me and said the same thing. No screw bashed me the whole time I was in prison for kidnapping that judge.

I eventually found out that George Burcheck had an understanding of what being in prison was all about. He once said to me, 'I spent three years as a Russian prisoner of war in a German prison camp. I was five and a half stone. They fed us turnips; they would just throw the turnips over the fence to us. That was all we had to eat for three years – turnips and water.'

If Pentridge didn't, for me, live up to its name of being the Bash House, it did live up to another of its nicknames – the College of Knowledge.

H Division had a library that had a four-rung bookshelf with all sorts of books on it.

I picked up the first one and read that, and eventually I read every book on the shelf, so they started getting in other books for me to read. I read all the Falconhurst books by Kyle Onstott – *Drum*, *Mandingo* and *Master of Falconhurst*. I learned the science of necropsy and all about embalming bodies.

I got the complete works of BF Skinner – Burrhus Frederic Skinner. Some people say he was the most influential psychologist of the twentieth century. I wanted to study psychology to stay psychologically on top of everyone in H Division, so I read everything by BF Skinner.

He was the person who thought up the three colours for traffic lights: green for 'go', amber for 'get ready to stop' and red for 'stop'. Now, every day, billions of people all over the world respond to those colours. He was an expert in people's responses to all sorts of things. All up, BF Skinner wrote twenty-one books, and I read all of them.

He had a daughter who committed suicide when she was twenty-seven and who was a gifted psychologist too. She wrote a thesis in which she explained how her father had brought her up to the sound of bells, a bit like Pavlov and his dogs.

One bell meant it was morning and she had to prepare cereal for breakfast. There was another that meant she had to make toast, and another that meant she had to make coffee. Another bell told her to have a bath, and then there was another to tell her to get out of the bath and dry herself. There was also another bell to tell her to play the piano, one to tell her to play the clarinet and another that told her to play the cello. She'd play softball, walk the dog, and all to the sound of these bells. She had more than three hundred things she did to the sound of bells.

In the end, she became terrified of the sound of the bells triggering her to do something. She might be at work and hear a sound like the bell for her to get in the shower, and she would have to get in the shower; or she'd be walking down the street and hear another bell and have a mad urge to go and play the piano. So, she committed suicide because she could no longer stand the pressure of living with this terror.

Even though one of BF Skinner's goals was to stop humanity destroying itself, he copped a lot of criticism in the medical world for the way he treated his daughter. They said he was inhumane.

I used to put a lot of what BF Skinner wrote into practice when I had the Overcoat Gang War going on in H Division.

I read a lot of other books too and, I suppose, I really educated myself while in H Division. I certainly learned a lot about the world that I hadn't known before I went in, and that a lot of people outside didn't know.

One night when I was out of prison, Margaret and I were at home watching a movie. It was about Hitler's invasion of Russia during World War II and there was snow everywhere. Margaret piped up and asked, 'So, is this why they call it the Cold War?' And she was serious.

Whenever I tell that story, she counters it by saying I am the person who didn't know what 'self-centred' meant and so had to have it explained to him. Well, I wouldn't, would I? Never had a self-centred thought in my life before she told me what one was; or one after, for that matter.

Anyway, what I learned from BF Skinner proved pretty helpful in prison. I used a lot of mind control in the Overcoat Gang War to get the responses I wanted the most and to be in control of my enemies.

I used to convince them I could get out of my cell and into theirs. I also convinced them I could get hold of the screws' keys with their permission, and could open up their cells and bash them and no one would be any the wiser. That was because if they said they were bashed by Chopper at nine pm, when we were all locked up, no one would believe them.

You needed two sets of keys for the cell doors after lockdown, one of which was held by the governor of security. I made my enemies think I could get hold of both sets of keys.

I had a lot of enemies in Pentridge, because even your friends are enemies when you're in jail. This was something I was to discover applied even in the case of Jimmy Loughnan.

I was prepared to go to jail for trying to help Jimmy Loughnan get out of jail. That didn't stop him trying to kill me.

I had been waging a long and bloody battle in Pentridge. Jimmy Loughnan was part of my gang, the Overcoat Gang. We had homemade axes under overcoats we wore, and would go around the prison bashing people up. We basically took on the whole prison, but our main enemies were people like Piggy Palmer, and some of the other blokes from the Painters and Dockers. These blokes seemed to have it all sorted out in their favour at Pentridge. My friends and I in the Overcoat Gang decided we'd like a bit of action for ourselves.

The Overcoat Gang War, silly as it sounds, really started over a bunch of sausages. Piggy Palmer accused me of eating all the sausages meant for Christmas dinner in H Division in 1975. We were supposed to get two each, and I was in charge of preparing the food. Somehow, with all these blokes sitting around the Christmas dinner table, salivating at the thought of two sausages each, when the food turned up there were no sausages.

Piggy was not amused. I tried to explain that, before I became the SNAG, as in sensitive new age guy, I am today, I wasn't that attached to sausages. Well, not attached enough to eat sixty of them in one sitting.

To this day, I don't know what happened to the sausages. I think they fell off the tray as a couple of prisoners from A Division brought the food down, and were replaced with cold corned beef. Whatever happened, I was not believed. Things were said that day that could never be unsaid.

A Rubicon was crossed.

The Overcoat Gang War had begun.

It went on for a long time: pretty much until they built the Jika Jika high-security unit, where they could keep us all separate. And it was brutal. It made all the stuff that went on between the Morans and Carl Williams look like a friendly barbecue, with or without sausages. Because it happened inside Pentridge, it didn't get the coverage those gangland killings did, but it was dog eat dog and then some.

We were outnumbered in the Overcoat Gang, but were always prepared to go that one step further than our enemies were.

And we had a bit of support in some interesting places. Jimmy Quinn was the governor of Pentridge. He was a real gentleman from the old school, was Governor Quinn. For a start, he was a mate of my dad's, so that helped me a bit. Also, sometime in the past, he had been bashed by my enemy who can't be named here, an unfortunate event that had left poor old Gentleman Jim with a broken nose.

Jimmy Quinn and I got on really well. He would arrange for me to be escorted to his office in handcuffs, but, once we got inside his office, off came the cuffs and out came the tea and biscuits.

There was also the suggestion that a bomb that went off in A Division might have had links to the Overcoat Gang War; a bit like the way when a bomb goes off somewhere in the world today, they say it might have links to Osama Bin Laden. After the bomb went off in A Division, injuring Piggy Palmer and a bloke called Neil Bugg, Trevor Taylor got transferred from that division to H Division.

If you listened to all the gossip, Taylor might have been acting on orders from Jimmy Loughnan, who might have been acting on orders from Chopper Read. Never listen to gossip, especially if you haven't got all of your ears.

I would like to make an apology to Neil Bugg, though. He was just an innocent bystander; no member of the Overcoat Gang had anything against Neil Bugg.

Another thing that Jimmy Loughnan and I liked doing was getting blokes to munch on razor blades. We'd pick a bloke who hadn't shown us enough respect – 'putting holes in his manners', we called it. Anyway, after giving the bloke with poor manners a belting, I would hold a knife to his throat and Jimmy would force him to put a razor blade in his mouth and bite on it. Blood would go everywhere.

The razor blade was a favourite weapon of mine. I would attach one to the end of a toothbrush. To carry out this bit of Chopper Read ingenuity, you needed just three things: a razor blade, obviously; a toothbrush, also obviously; and a cigarette lighter. None of the above was hard to obtain in Pentridge. Don't try this at home, kiddies, but first, take your toothbrush and hold it above the flame of the cigarette lighter. When the plastic starts to melt, stick the razor blade into it. When the plastic hardens again, you have a highly lethal implement. Just swishing it around with a delicate movement of the wrist can do a lot of damage to an enemy's good looks.

We had a lot of weapons to hide under our overcoats as the war raged on. We would get screwdrivers and sharpen them up. We had homemade axes, iron bars and garden spades. The prison kitchen wasn't a bad place to get stuff, either – butcher's knives, icepicks, you name it, we had it. They say necessity is the mother of invention. Well, we invented quite a few necessities in our mother of a war. It was complete madness, really, and in the end, I reckon, we broke the will of a lot of people to resist us. We could put shit in their food, we could make them eat razor blades, we could hit them over the head with blunt instruments, we could slash their faces.

Jimmy Price, Jimmy Loughnan, Chopper Read, Amos Atkinson . . . we were probably all quite mad at the time. And, for the most part, we were all highly loyal to each other back then, though things changed afterwards.

Speaking of Amos Atkinson, how's this for a sign of his great love and affection for Mark Brandon 'Chopper' Read? In 1978, he took thirty hostages at the Italian Waiters Club and said that if I wasn't let out of Pentridge, he would start shooting people. That would have put a few of them off their spaghetti bolognaise and chianti. Anyway, the siege lasted a few hours and then it was over. Amos got five years.

Amos Atkinson became a member of another little club I had going in Pentridge – the Van Gogh Club. For those who might not know, Vincent Van Gogh was a Dutch painter who some people thought was a little bit mad. He cut off the fleshy lobe of his left ear and then did a self-portrait with his head all bandaged up. Amos Atkinson cut off both his ears in 1979. After

I had done it, a few blokes started taking it up as a good idea.

And as for Garry David – or Garry David Webb, he had a few identities as well as personalities – well, he took the Van Gogh Club into a whole new dimension. He cut off his cock – three times.

The first time he cut it off, the screws grabbed it and took him and his cock off to the hospital, where they sewed it back on. Then he cut it off a second time and put it on the cistern of his toilet. The screws picked it up again and took it off to the hospital, where they again sewed it back on. When he cut it off the third time, he made sure the screws didn't get hold of it. He flushed it down the toilet. The screws took him off to hospital but this time without his cock, which by now was well and truly on its way to the sewage works at Werribee.

Without his cock, poor old Garry David was now in more shit than a Werribee duck. When he came back to prison, he and I ended up in the showers together. I kept telling myself, 'Don't look down, don't look down; whatever you do, don't look down, Chopper.'

Well, of course, I had to look down, didn't I?

And there it was – the strangest, funniest, saddest thing you've ever seen. Sticking out of the end of what was left of Garry David's cock was three inches of plastic tubing. And on the end of it was a little nozzle, like the ones you find on wine casks. That was his replacement dick, so, every time he went to the toilet, he had to twist the little nozzle.

Keen observers in the showers also noticed he still had his Salada crackers – his knackers. That meant he could still get an erection, so everyone was sending him *Playboy* magazines, but all the poor bugger had was this bit of plastic tube and a nozzle at the end of it.

Garry David was famous for always saying, 'I will not be told what to do.' So much so, we pretty much renamed him Garry 'I Will Not Be Told What to Do' David. He lived up to his name and died because of it.

After the first time he ate a piece of the mop bucket, he was told not to do it again because they had had to cut away part of his intestine to get it out.

'I will not be told what to do,' he said.

And he ate a bit more of the mop bucket, and so they had to remove a bit more of his intestine, and they said, Garry, you can't do it again because there is so little of your intestine left that you will die.

'I will not be told what to do,' was his answer to that and, of course, he did it again, and, of course, he died.

He became quite famous around the world for all his self-harm. There's even a chapter on him in a book called *The Odd Brain: Mysteries of Our Weird and Wonderful Brains Explained*.

The author claims that Garry David ate glass, drank Brasso, sulfuric acid and the contents of a nine-volt battery. He stuck fish bones in his eyes and amputated his penis, his nipples and one of his heels. He severed his Achilles tendon and nailed his feet to the floor, injected urine into his body, extracted blood from his arm, using a fountain pen, and stuck razor blades up his bum.

An Australian country and western singer by the name of Gene Bradley Fisk wrote a song called 'On the Run' that was based on Garry David's letters. Apparently, Fisk gave Garry David a copy of a David Allan Coe biography, to encourage him to stop hacking away at his vitals. David Allan Coe is an American country and western singer who spent a lot of his life in jail, and maybe even on death row for a while, but still managed to have a musical career. I was a fan of his for a while there, too. Getting Garry David to follow David Allan Coe, to see there could be a world outside chopping yourself up, was a nice idea at the time, but, once again, he wouldn't be told what to do, by either a doctor, a screw, or a country and western singer.

But what to do with Garry caused a big to-do when he was about to be released. The Victorian Government eventually brought in the Community Protection Act, to keep him in jail after he'd served his fourteen years for attempted murder while robbing a pizza place in Rye. All up, you'd have to say that Garry 'I Won't Be Told What to Do' David was a complete maniac – well, complete except for the bits he kept cutting off.

Anyway, back to the Overcoat Gang, with me, Amos and Jimmy and a few others, and our homemade axes. While I knew we were winning the war, what I was really looking for was a coup de grâce, a grand plan. I love grand plans.

I had an idea to lock all the screws in the scullery. We would take all their keys off them and stuff matches in the locks so they couldn't use anything else to get out. Then we would get into all the cells, and also go down to the labour yard, and we would stab every prisoner in the spine with an icepick, render them cripples. They would be like jelly.

Amos Atkinson got out of H Division shortly after I'd announced that plan, and I think he was glad of that. I don't think Jimmy liked my idea and so that's why he decided to stab me. There is a story that he had been told there was a contract from someone in the Painters and Dockers to have me killed and he was trying to take advantage of that. But my belief is that he tried to kill me because he didn't like this grand plan of mine to win the Overcoat Gang War once and for all.

One day, he came up to me and started punching me in the guts.

I said, 'It's a bit early in the day for kung fu isn't it, Jimmy?'

I said that because all I could feel at first was this whack in the guts, but I did notice, even the first time, a bit of coldness, from the steel.

He stabbed me three times before I realised what he was doing.

I looked down and could see blood on my highly polished shoes.

I said, 'Jimmy, if you keep on stabbing me, you're going to kill me.'

I grabbed him and put him in a headlock, and kissed him on the head.

He pushed me back, and stabbed me twice more.

All up, he stabbed me five times. I know that in other publications and in the movie *Chopper*, it has been said he stabbed me seven times. But I'm the one with the scars and I've counted them. There are five.

After the fifth time, I grabbed him by the throat and pushed him up against the wall. But because I had been stabbed five times, all the muscles in my stomach had stopped working, so I couldn't stand up.

I fell over backwards and Jimmy Loughnan's head ended up in my lap. Then, he must have realised what he was doing, and got the screws to come and assist me. If he hadn't done that, I would probably have died.

So, on the same day he tried to kill me, he saved my life. He was a bloody schizo, Jimmy; half of him wanted to kill me and half of him didn't.

So, anyway, I was taken off for treatment, and all the questioning began and Jimmy tried to make out he was acting in self-defence. He cut himself to make it look like I had tried to stab him first. The reason he did that was that he knew that if he was found guilty of trying to kill me, he would be sent back to J Ward in Ararat, and he didn't want to go there again.

In the end, another prisoner, Gregory John 'Bluey' Brazel, took the blame for him. He was an interesting character, 'Bluey' Brazel. He and I share a birthday, 17 November 1954. The first thing that got him into prison was having to do two years for being in contempt of court, in 1983. But he had an interesting history even before that. When he was in the Australian Army, he took five privates hostage during a training exercise. Apparently, a few shots were fired before he was persuaded to give the hostages back.

Thankfully, no one got shot in the privates. Ha ha!

'Bluey' Brazel has been convicted of three murders: those of the prostitutes Sharon Taylor and Roslyn Hayward, and he also fatally shot a woman, the owner of a hardware store, during an armed hold-up.

That was in 1982, but he didn't confess to the crime until 2005.

Once, he took a prison guard hostage – that was in 1991, when he heard he was going to be taken back to Pentridge. In 2003, he tricked some little old lady into putting $30,000 into his betting account while he was in prison. Then, in 2006, he got $12,000 as compensation for being bashed in prison.

Anyway, he took the rap for Jimmy Loughnan having stabbed me. But not before the police turned up with a statement ready for me to sign, saying that I had stabbed Jimmy first.

They wanted to charge me with attempted murder.

I made a statement contradicting that, saying that I hadn't tried to kill Jimmy before he tried to kill me. When the charge of attempted murder got to court, I blew the whole thing up into La La land – it went nowhere.

I guess Jimmy and I remained friends after that, in a funny sort of way.

In 1983, I saw him out the front of B Division and he squirmed a bit because he thought I was going to hit him.

And I said, 'Don't worry about me hitting you, Jimmy, I am not going to do that.'

Instead, I put my arms around him and kissed him. I think he might have had tears in his eyes as he walked away.

I once said to him, 'Your life will get you in the end.'

Jimmy Loughnan died along with four other prisoners, in the fire at Jika Jika in 1987.

Just before he died, he came up to me and said, 'Are you up for a bit of fun, Chopper?'

I asked him what he meant by that.

He said there was going to be a riot in Jika Jika, the $7 million prison they had built at Pentridge, which had a closed-in roof so people couldn't escape by helicopter, and all these automated doors and a controlled climate. It was a prison within a prison that was meant for all the hardened crims.

The prisoners were staging the riot in protest against the inhuman way they were being treated in Jika Jika.

I told Jimmy the best thing to do would be to set fire to the pneumatic doors because the tubes in them would melt.

What I didn't bother telling him was that when the doors locked when the pneumatic mechanism melted, they couldn't be opened. And what I also didn't bother telling him was that the air-conditioning would shut down.

All five of them died of smoke inhalation. They were trying to get the water out of their toilets so that they could get air that way, but it didn't work and they all choked to death on the smoke.

Jimmy Loughnan wasn't a druggie or anything like that, and just saw himself as an armed robber. He did a few jobs for Jockey Smith, and was a gunman around the Richmond area. I don't think he had any great ambition in the criminal world.

He had a funny walk, did Jimmy – he was a bit of a spring-handled jack. He had absolutely no coordination at all and if you threw a tennis ball at him, he couldn't catch it.

When we tried to bash Dennis Allen, Peter Allen's brother, Jimmy would have taken half a dozen swings at him and didn't hit him once. It was left to me to hit Dennis, something I did with a rolling pin, around nineteen times.

We egg-shelled his skull, meaning it split like an eggshell cracks.

That happened down in the dungeon in B Division in 1975 and, probably understandably, Dennis Allen didn't like me much afterwards either. I reckon since then he must have spent thousands of dollars trying to have me killed.

Obviously, he never succeeded.

In my first book, *Chopper from the Inside*, I revealed how I had always managed to elude Dennis and his murderous plans. I had a spy in his camp: a woman by the name of Tracy Glenda Warren. I am not sure why she confided in me with all the pillow talk that Dennis Allen confided in her. We weren't in any sort of relationship with each other; I guess it just added some excitement to Tracy's life.

Dennis Allen wasn't all that good with money, even though he made plenty of it from selling heroin. I came up with a cunning plan to relieve him of a lot of it, and all without the use of even one gas bottle. I would have some of my allies approach him with their own cunning plan of how to have me killed. Allen would hand them an amount of money and, after they had taken their cut, to which they were perfectly entitled, they would then hand the rest over to me.

Dennis Allen shot dead a bloke by the name of Wayne Stanhope, who I had met in prison in 1983. When Wayne got out, he befriended Dennis Allen, apparently not knowing that Dennis and I weren't exactly on each other's Christmas card list. I had been transferred to the old jail in Geelong and, one day, Wayne told Dennis Allen he had gone down there to visit me.

Soon after, Wayne was dead, shot while changing a record.

I didn't last all that long in the Geelong jail. The prison officials thought I always seemed to have got too many chocolates and other goodies from the canteen without actually purchasing them.

Like Pentridge, the Geelong jail has been shut down and people can have guided tours of it. And the tour guides always mention Chopper Read having been in there as one of the main attractions. Funny how going on a tour of a prison interests people. Academics even write long-winded papers about it.

It's got a bit of history about it, the Geelong jail. The poor buggers who built it were all convicts. They were kept as prisoners in a sailing ship on Corio Bay, at the bottom end of Bellarine Street in Geelong. Every morning, they would have to get up, be taken ashore, and march up Bellarine Street to work on the prison. Then, at night, they would be marched back down Bellarine Street and put on the ship. This went on until they finished the jail and were all moved in there.

I am not sure how I would have felt if I had had to help build Pentridge. Mind you, I did watch with great interest as they wasted $7 million of taxpayers' money building Jika Jika only to have to close it down. And now, of course, they're turning Pentridge into a residential area. I can tell you that it really is messing with the minds of a few former residents, as you will see when you get to the chapter about Margaret's and my wedding.

After the bashing of Dennis Allen in B Division's dungeon, a few of the people from H Division were sent up to Beechworth Prison. Peter Allen escaped from Beechworth soon after he heard that I was coming up there. He's the only person in Australia ever acquitted of escaping from jail on the basis of self-defence.

One time, Jimmy Loughnan and I tried to break out of B Division. We were up in the ceiling above the B Division library, had lollies and cordial and were set to go. But, even before we had got out of the place, Jimmy had eaten all the lollies and drunk all the cordial, and so he needed to have a widdle. He widdled into his coat but some of the urine went running down the wall. So, there was this yellow urine running down the walls of the library in B Division and we were discovered. It was a debacle.

In the end, I couldn't wait to be caught.

But I've learned recently that that failed escape attempt might have been the reason that Bon Scott from AC/DC wrote the song 'Jailbreak'. When I think about it, that could be true because I once met Bon Scott at the Southside Six Hotel. This was a place I used to go to watch live music in Melbourne. Remember Kush, with Jeff Duff as the lead singer? Yeah, you're old, aren't you?

Me aged twenty months.

Mornington State School, Grade 5, 1965: I am in the second row,
third from the right.

75764 © Newspix / News Ltd

Tools of the trade. Notice I'm not wearing
my 'knuckle busters' in this shot.

Margaret and me at Bendigo Prison before
getting out and going to Tassie.

The day I was given the Governor's Pleasure in Tasmania.

Margaret and my dad.

Me and my sister.

Margaret's favourite uncle, Charlie, with our pit
bull terrier cross, Mr Nibbles.

Margaret and me on our wedding day.

My wedding day.

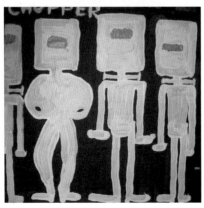

The painting I did of our wedding: Margaret,
me, the best man and Adam Cullen.

I am told Mick Gatto now has one of my paintings hanging in his gym.

Anthony Kiedis, the lead singer of The Red Hot Chili Peppers, and I compare tattoos.

Jimmy Barnes always has me backstage when he
plays in Melbourne.

Left to right: Dave Hedgcock, me and Ivan Rakitić. Have
a guess how old Dave is — if you guess right, I bet you
wouldn't have the guts to tell him to his face!

This is Bob Jones, the *soke* of Zen Do Kai
karate. You wouldn't believe how old he is.

Left to right: Ivan Rakitić, me and Richard Norton.

Me and Margaret.

Some more of my artwork.

Me and Frankie Waghorn. We've been friends since the age of
nine and we've never had a cross word.

105191© Newspix / News Ltd

Here I am on *Elle McFeast Live* killing off Libbi Gorr's
TV career.

Roy's christening. He is six months old.

Four-year-old Roy at kindergarten.

Roy with our dog, Kyser.

Roy with Uncle Ron.

Dight Falls: Roy and me pretending to fish.

Me, Roy and Mick Gatto.

Jeff Duff had a deep voice but there wasn't much else that was manly about him. He was a pretty flamboyant sort of character. He used to get around on stage dressed in a mink stole and fishnet stockings, and stuff like that. His first album, in 1975, was called *Snow White and the Eight Straights*.

Well, anyway, this night at the Southside Six, Jeff Duff introduced me to Bon Scott. I didn't think a real lot of it at the time, as I used to get introduced to a lot of musicians back then. But it would be kind of interesting if Bon Scott had remembered me from that night, heard the story of Jimmy and me trying to get out of prison, and wrote 'Jailbreak' for us. It would be a nice way for Jimmy to be remembered.

Jimmy came from a pretty swish family from around Richmond. They've named a street and a hall – Loughnan Hall – after them there. His family used to run Richmond, being well into politics. Jimmy's grandfather, James Richard Loughnan, was the mayor. While Jimmy's father, Richard James Loughnan, wasn't all that into politics himself, he was still very well connected. Clyde Holding always promised the Loughnans he would get Jimmy out of jail if he ever became premier of Victoria. Holding was leader of the Labor Opposition in Victoria for ten years before he went off to Federal Parliament. He never got elected premier, so was never able to honour that promise to the Loughnans to get Jimmy out of jail.

Jimmy was a good friend of mine and was also the bloke who stabbed me. But for a lot of reasons it would be good if it was true that Bon Scott wrote that song about the pair of us. For a start, I reckon Jimmy would much prefer to have an AC/DC song than a street as a memorial to him. And it would be nice to think that, long before I made my own records, I had inspired someone like Bon Scott. Also, AC/DC was the first-ever band that Margaret went to see. She saw them in a hall in Melbourne somewhere, when they were just starting out. As well, lo and behold, all these years on, AC/DC is our son Roy's favourite band. We took him to see them when they toured Australia in 2010. We even bought him a pair of those little red horns that Angus wears.

Anyway, I started out telling you how Chopper Read went from being a Seventh Day Adventist to a bloke doing time in Pentridge, and ended up talking about AC/DC. Life's a journey!

Jimmy Loughnan turning on me did really mess me up physically and mentally. Here I was, serving seventeen years for trying to get him out of prison, and he stabbed me.

I lost all sorts of bits of my body – spleen, gall bladder, intestine. After they operated on me, the next day, they found me on the hospital floor, doing push-ups. I wanted to prove to the bastard that, while he had stabbed me, he hadn't really got at me and I wanted to be fighting fit to get back at him. I ripped open all the stitches they'd just put in me to hold me together, so the doctors had to sew me back up again.

Despite my bravado, I did become a physical wreck. Before that incident, I was 115 kilos of muscle. Jimmy Loughnan had turned me into an 88-kilo weakling.

There are so many stories about my time in prison, especially in Pentridge.

I made friends, I lost friends.

I made enemies and I've kept most of them.

I think I completely lost Amos Robert Atkinson as a friend in 1984, when he got a clock radio sent to him in Jika Jika. I thought I was just being funny when I called out to him something along the lines of 'White man make big magic in little box.' Amos was an Aborigine. He dropped the radio and it broke, and he sooked in his cell for ages.

There was another episode that probably cruelled the friendship a bit too. When I was out of jail in 1987, a time of great madness and paranoia in my life, I went to his house early one morning and fired three shots into the air. He called me a mad bastard and told me to piss off. I suppose I would have said that too if someone had done it to me.

I've got another favourite Amos Robert Atkinson story.

There was a little Lebanese cake shop owner who got bashed up by an Aussie butcher shop owner. Amos was a friend of the Lebanese cake shop owner, so he went around and pistol whipped the Australian butcher and said to leave the cake shop owner alone. The cake shop owner told Amos he was eternally grateful to him and promised to help him any way he could if Amos ever got into trouble.

Well, not long after, Amos found himself in trouble with a gun-toting Lebanese person, a huge man. The cake shop owner heard about this and said to Amos, 'Are you in trouble with Louie?' Amos said he was.

The cake shop owner told him to come around to the cake shop that night. Amos did and there was Louie, with a lot of other Lebanese people. He was on the phone to someone, talking away in Lebanese. He was as white as a ghost and shaking. And when Amos walked in, he just about saluted him.

Amos asked the cake shop owner what was going on. He said that Louie was on the phone to people in Lebanon and had been told by someone there that unless he apologised to Amos Atkinson immediately, everyone with the last name of Ferrar would be dead the next day.

It turned out that the little cake shop owner was the nephew of Yasser Arafat. There are, apparently, a lot of Yasser Arafat's relatives living in Melbourne and, at that time, as head of the Palestine Liberation Organisation, he was not a bloke you'd want to mess with.

There are a few more Amos Robert Atkinson stories from the years in Pentridge, but I reckon that one takes the cake. There are plenty of other stories, too, from what I would call the wild days of the young Chopper Read.

Some I've written about before and some I haven't.

Some are the truth, the whole truth and nothing but the truth.

Some aren't.

One day not that long ago, when I was down in Tasmania visiting my son Charlie, he turned to me and said, 'How many people have you killed, Dad?'

I said, 'What made you ask that – your mother hasn't let you watch the *Chopper* movie, has she?'

He said she had.

'That's why I divorced your mother,' I said to him.

But it's a question I've been asked a lot of times, and that I've answered a lot of times, over the years.

Of course, the answers mightn't have always been the same. A lot of the time it can depend on who is asking the question. If it was the homicide squad, you might have a different answer from the one you'd give to a mate in the pub or write in a book.

The answer also depends on how you define killing someone. Is pulling the trigger the same as being in the room when someone else pulls the trigger to kill someone?

I guess the answer I'd give these days is around four or five people.

There was Sammy the Turk – self-defence. There was that bloke who had me digging my own grave – self-defence. There was the bloke who Dave the Jew had shot and bashed, and who begged me to put him out of his misery, so that was more an act of kindness than murder.

There was also the bloke I shot while he was in a phone booth. I've probably embellished that story a bit over the years.

I was asked by a certain tall member of the Painters and Dockers to shoot this bloke, and I did, in the leg. Only problem was, the bullet hit his femoral artery, so blood went everywhere. Over the years, I've said I left him there in the phone booth to die, but the truth is, he was found outside a shopping centre. Someone had taken him there in the hope he'd be found and get some help. He didn't get found in time. When you get shot in the femoral artery, you need help pretty quickly.

And then there was another incident in Pentridge, involving a bloody paedophile.

He had only been out of prison for a short time, after serving a sentence for rape after he abducted a three-year-old girl and tried to have sex with her. Her vagina wasn't big enough, so he cut her open with the lid of a jam tin. It was a disgusting crime and he was a disgusting person. He was supposed to be held in protective custody because a lot of people in prison don't like paedophiles; especially paedophiles who cut open three-year-old girls with the lid of a jam tin.

One day, Mad Charlie and I were walking past his cell and noticed that his door was open and there was no one else around. So, we decided to administer a bit of justice of our own.

We jumped this bloke, bashed him and knocked him to the ground, tied him up, and just kept on bashing him till he was knocked out. While he was lying on the ground, we jumped off his bed and onto his head. Because he was lying on a concrete floor and we were jumping off the bed, we egg-shelled his skull and broke a lot of other bones in his body. We kept doing this and eventually he died. We then grabbed a sheet off his bed and strung him up so that it looked like he had committed suicide by hanging himself.

As Mad Charlie and I were heading back to our cells, I do remember saying to him that we should probably have untied his hands, because it's pretty hard to smash your own head in, break every bone in your body, then hang yourself when you've got your hands tied together behind your back.

The bloke was found and carted away, but nothing ever came back on Charlie and me. From memory, the coroner was the visiting magistrate at Pentridge, and he and I got on pretty well. I think he liked my sense of humour. I was up before him just about every month for bashing someone but, of course, none of the victims would give a statement against me, so I would get off every time. And, of course, this bloody paedophile wasn't able to give a statement, so, yeah; I think it all just got sorted. I still get a Christmas card every year from that little girl's family, though.

So, if you weren't a copper and asked me nicely how many people I've killed, maybe four or five.

H DIVISION wasn't the only place I spent a lot of time when I was in Pentridge. I was also put into Jika Jika, the state-of-the-art high-security prison built in the 1980s.

Some people say it was built especially for me; or, at least, to put an end to the Overcoat Gang Wars. I was the first inmate in Jika Jika and they were watching every move I made, because they could: it was all very high tech.

It sat at the end of what they called the Pentridge alphabet:

A: Short- and long-term prisoners, good behaviour
B: Long-term prisoners with behaviour problems
C: Closed down in 1971
D: Remand prisoners
E: Similar to A

F: Remand and short-term
G: Psychiatric problems
H: High security, discipline and protection
J: Long-term with record of good behaviour
Jika Jika: Maximum security risk and protection.

Jika Jika was taken from the name of the tribe that first inhabited the area, the Jaga Jaga. Apparently, a lot of Aboriginal people were horrified that one of their sacred names would be applied to such a place. I would have been too if I was an Aborigine.

The exercise yard was enclosed so that nobody could escape by helicopter. Four blokes did escape, though, if not by helicopter. A couple of screws were charged after that escape for not doing their jobs properly and the whole jail went on strike. It was not the happiest of places for anyone, really – prisoners or screws.

Margaret says that once a visit was over, you, the visitor, would hear this eerie clatter of the door behind you and that was it. I felt very cut off from the real world – if you could call the rest of Pentridge the real world. It was a prison within a prison. Eventually, about fifty people ended up in there.

Anyway, while I was in Jika Jika, a few good-hearted types in some government department decided to make a documentary about some of our Victorian prisons. It might have been because, I seem to remember, the jails were getting bad press at the time. There would be an incident, a riot or something, which would be described as a one-off by the government or the prison department. But, of course, they weren't one-offs. Blokes were getting bashed all the time. It was out of control.

I also remember the Prison Reform Society was getting pretty active around that time, with the opening of not just Jika Jika but a similar prison in Sydney at Long Bay, called Katingal.

Both were supposed to be escape proof. No one told Russell 'Mad Dog' Cox that. He got out of Katingal. He was out for eleven years after that, and even managed not just to win Lotto, but to collect the $15,000. Eventually, he was turned in by Raymond John Denning, a real dog of an act.

Before I actually got to meet Russell Cox, in H Division in 1991, there had been whispering campaigns about the two of us not liking each other very much. But, apart from the fact that he was a vegetarian – he made vegetarian curries that would napalm your mouth on the way in and blow your arse to kingdom come on the way out – we had a lot in common. We were both well read. We both had a very low opinion of a lot of people in the criminal world.

I, of course, have long had a low opinion of the Sydney criminal element, but Russell Cox is the exception there. I would go as far as to call him one of Australia's greatest bank robbers and I devoted a whole chapter to Russell Cox in my first book.

I noticed he was in the news again early in 2010, when police apparently questioned him over the death of Brian Kane, Victoria's oldest unsolved murder. Last year, police doubled the reward for information that identified the killer to $100,000.

Anyway, back in Jika Jika, there was all this bad press about prisons and prison officers. The credits on the documentary say the Victorian Law Foundation and the Victorian Institute of Law were part of the project, and that it was produced for Curriculum Services Unit, Legal Studies, by the Television Section, Education Department of Victoria. Who knows who they were?

Anyhow, whoever was making the documentary, they had the full cooperation of the prison bosses. And these prison bosses must have decided it would be a good idea to include an interview with Chopper Read, me being one of the most highly regarded prisoners in Pentridge. So, this nice lady, Diane O'Connor, sat me down on a bench in Jika Jika and we had a chat about this and that. I didn't really know who Diane O'Connor was. Someone might have told me she came from the University of Melbourne.

Anyway, I still have a copy of our filmed cosy little chat. It was a video back then, I guess. I've got it on a DVD now, with my picture on the front. I was in my blue overalls and white prison shoes. My ears were gone, as they'd been cut off, but I had these nice little sideburns. Everyone had sideburns back then, so I probably reckoned I should have them too. I looked quite handsome, I thought.

And, looking back at the conversation I had with Diane, I guess a few things have changed.

The sideburns have gone! Also, I told her I wasn't interested in getting married or having a tribe of kids.

While I haven't got a tribe of kids, I've got two: little Charlie, down in Hobart, and Roy, who lives with Margaret and me in Collingwood. And I am, of course, married now, for the second time, to Margaret. Two's enough for me in that particular department, too.

As I said, I don't know what the original documentary was used for or where it got shown. But if someone out there does, drop me a note.

The transcript has never been reproduced in full anywhere before, so here's a little exclusive for you. Happy reading.

Mark Read: I was sent to Jika Jika from H Division because I was a high security risk. I was attacking other prisoners. So they sent me here to put an end to it.

Diane O'Connor: Where had you been before this?

MR: I had been in H Division for about a year and a half, two years, and before that, oh no I was in G Division for ten months, and they brought me here to bring an end to a lot of trouble.

DOC: What sort of trouble?

MR: Oh well, um, since 1975 I have been involved in internal, oh, feuds with other prisoners, sort of like a gang war with other prisoners since 1975 . . . a lot of trouble and a lot of people got hurt.

DOC: Why do you think they would build a place like this?

MR: I suppose they need some place to put the maximum security prisoners. They haven't got enough room to put them elsewhere because trouble erupts wherever you put them so it is best to put them here out of harm's way.

DOC: So how successful do you think it is?

MR: Oh well, it is no greater success than any other division in Pentridge. Just as much trouble can erupt here as can erupt anywhere else, just that here they can isolate the trouble. The trouble is more isolated. There is nothing that will put an end to trouble but here they have the trouble all in one spot.

DOC: Do you think that for you personally anything has changed by being here?

MR: It hasn't changed me personally but it may change other people. It hasn't done me any good or given me any benefit, personally.

DOC: Have any incidents occurred here involving you?

MR: Violent? There have been violent occurrences here, um, involving me. But they will put an end to that now just by putting me in isolation. Yeah.

DOC: What sort of other prisoners come here?

MR: Oh, child tamperists, rapists, murderers, police informers, people who are on high protection, you know, who are hated throughout the jail, um, various psychos of one form or another. People who are the greatest risk to cause the most trouble in one form or another come here.

DOC: What did you do originally to get into jail?

MR: I attacked Judge Martin in the County Court on 26 January 1978. I was trying to get my mate out of J Ward Ararat Mental Hospital but I was apprehended and brought to Pentridge and they give me seventeen and a half years for me trouble and it has been going on ever since, trouble, trouble, trouble.

DOC: I noticed that you did something with your ears, can you relate that story.

MR: Yeah, I cut 'em off with a . . . I went to the Classification Committee and I asked them to put me in another division and they told me I would stay in H Division indefinitely. So I went back to the yard and I got a razor blade and, I will be perfectly honest with you, a lot of people think I cut them off myself, but I got someone else to cut them off for me. Another prisoner and he wrapped it up in a bit of toilet paper not to cut his own hand and I sat there like that (folds arms) and he started cutting off this ear here (indicates right ear) and he's cutting like a piece of bread, cutting through and the blood is spurting out and he got that one off and he proceeded to be sick and I said, 'Well, cut the other one off as well,' so he's started hacking the other one off because it was an old razor blade and they both come off and I put me hands over me ears and it sounded terrible because it sounded like running a fingernail down tin when the razor blade was going right through, going through gristle and the blood was spurting out and, um, I put my hands over me ears and it sounded like I was listening to the trickling of water, but it was trickles of blood and I looked down at the ground and me ears were doing an Irish jig on the floor. And I walked up and down and I didn't know what to do, I thought I was going to have a cold shower and I thought that would make the blood go away because I knew Van Gogh cut his off and I thought if he could do it then, I could do it now. And the blood just wouldn't stop coming out so I had to knock up and ask for medical attention. Then I went completely off my head after that, I . . . they had to take me to hospital. And I was there for three weeks and they put me in G Division, the psychiatric division.

DOC: What reasons did you have for doing that?

MR: Oh, I don't know, I just, err, I thought at that time, at that moment it was the smartest thing to do, I wouldn't do it again, I couldn't do it again. The thing is at that moment I thought it was a wise move. I was off me head.

DOC: A wise move for anything in particular?

MR: I thought it would get me to J Ward and if it got me to J Ward I could be with me friends because at that time most of my friends were in J Ward Ararat and I wanted to get up there because if [I] could get up there I would be sweet. Everything would be going well.

DOC: That sounds amazing. How do you think they would go about saying that someone is insane?

MR: Well, if someone acts abnormally they bring a psychiatrist down to interview them and the psychiatrist certifies you and sends you to jail at Ararat. But I can't get certified, nothing I can do can certify me. I suppose a lot of people would like that. I just can't seem to do anything right. Everything I do they say, 'Oh, that's perfectly sane.' You know, I cut me ears off and it was considered quite normal.

DOC: So do you think you're perfectly sane?

MR: No, I know that I am not perfectly sane. I've self-mutilated me body and I've done a lot of things that people would consider insane and I was born autistic, which a lot of people don't understand. See, an autistic child he's got no real under-standing of right or wrong or fear or danger. An autistic child will walk into a fire or walk into water . . . you've got to keep an eye on him because he has no real understanding of danger, you know. So when I cut me ears off I didn't have any real understanding that I could bleed to death, or whether it would hurt. I didn't really feel any great pain because my mind was not really expecting any great pain. If my mind had of felt there would be pain involved in cutting me ears off I probably wouldn't have done it. I didn't think there was anything greatly serious about doing it. I do now, I do under-stand now that it was a terrible thing to do but at that time it didn't register on my brain.

DOC: Do you think yourself that being in a place like Jika Jika is going to help you when you leave?

MR: Oh, it will never help me. It might help other people in my position but it will never help me. All the jails and mental hospitals in the world wouldn't help me, I don't think. There's nothing much they can do apart from perform a lobotomy or a frontalectomy or something, there is nothing they can do to really change my position.

DOC: Why do you think that is?

MR: Well, I have been like this all my life.

DOC: You're not looking forward to something in the future?

MR: Well, there is nothing for me in the future. There is . . . I am not motivated by money. I don't want to get married and raise a tribe or a brood of children or lead a normal life. I have got no interest in that. I am stuck with what I've got.

DOC: How long will you spend in Jika Jika and what do you feel about that? What is it like being in here?

MR: I think I've got to spend the remaining part of my sentence in Jika Jika up until the last six months and they will probably put me elsewhere then to try and, you know, make me happy.

DOC: How does it feel being here, what is the atmosphere like?

MR: Well, it is a . . . I've never really given it any great thought at all until you mentioned it. Just a bit claustrophobic, a bit mechanical, you know. But it is no worse than any other division; it is just a $7 million comedy of errors.

DOC: Do you spend much time with the prisoners yourself? You mentioned that you are isolated. How do you find that?

MR: Well, I don't mind, I've got no great desire to mix with the other prisoners. I couldn't care less whether they lived or died. I am not a social climber. I have got no interest in being hail fellow well met with all the other prisoners. I couldn't care less if they built a little wooden dunny and suspended me above the jail and fed me once a day. I am here and I am not going to leave here until the end of me sentence and there is no use me worrying or complaining about what I am or what I am doing when I am here.

DOC: Do you think the prison officers are any different here to what they are elsewhere?

MR: Oh no, the prison officers are the same all over the jail, you know. That's an old fallacy about prison officers being great ogres, they're just ordinary human beings that have got a government job, a good, safe, government job, they're no different to any other prison officers. Except they don't use keys, they just push buttons.

DOC: So where do you think the main problems lie in prison for prisoners?

MR: The prisoners, well, they are the ones that make all the problems for themselves, you know. A prison officer is not going to stab you. A prison officer is not going to bomb your cell or get outside and rape or bash your wife or try and kill your kids. A prison officer is not going to manipulate you in prison to get you killed. If you are lying on the ground with a knife in your guts it's the prison officers who will apply oxygen, who will bandage you up and call the ambulance. The crim won't get on the phone and call the ambulance. So really the crims' main worry in jail is other crims, internal feuds within the jail. A prison officer is just an innocent bystander who's standing around watching it all and seems to be copping most of the flak.

DOC: How many incidents have there been of internal feuds?

MR: Oh, I think Pentridge would be the worst jail in Australia for internal feuds among prisoners, the prisoners are always at each other's throats. A gang war can last for five years, in fact it never really ends. It could go on for an indefinite period of time, you know. I was in one that lasted from 1975 until 1980 and the only reason it ended is because of this division. So I suppose this division has done something if it ended that. That was a very bloody little upset that went for a long time and a lot of people were involved.

DOC: What would motivate you to get involved in that gang war?

MR: Well, I just didn't like the faces of the people of the opposition. When I arrived in B Division they seemed to have everything under control, they were making all the home brews and getting all the dope in and organising everything and ran the place like kingpins and so I thought I would rectify the situation and we had some homemade axes made up in the engineer's shop and there was me and a couple of other friends and I made 'em wear overcoats and we had axes up our sleeves and we went around and dealt with the situation.

DOC: Do you think that the typical attitude to Pentridge prisoners is like they say?

MR: No, the Pentridge prisoner he whinges and squeals and screams and complains and moans and groans about his sad lot in life, his wife and children, his mother and father, they come and visit him and he sits there and he is currying sympathy and support by telling them how he is being brutally bashed and how he is being set up and how his letters are being torn up and his photographs are being torn up and he's not getting fed enough and he's not receiving the proper medical treatment and woe is me and what a terrible situation is this.

It is all a lot of crap because the prisoner's main worry is other prisoners. So he may get bashed by another prisoner, yet find it convenient to blame a prison officer for the bashing. Because if he blames a prison officer for the bashing, then he has a lever to threaten the prison officers with possible criminal charges against them for bashing him. Because I have bashed several prisoners myself and the only reason I have never been charged with it is because they have claimed prison officers have done the bashing, you know. It's a lot of rubbish. They're always whingeing and moaning and complaining.

DOC: If that's the case, would you rather be in Jika Jika or H Division?

MR: Well, I would rather [be] in H Division, I would rather be in the mainstream of the jail because I like being in the mainstream of the jail because there is more for me to do. I don't think the jail authorities would agree with what I would like to do but sitting here like this, it's very boring for me. I am constantly brooding and thinking about what I intend to do to certain people when I get out of here and it doesn't matter, all the jail and all the time in the world will never kill your hatred for certain people within the jail. You see, you make an enemy in jail and it seems to go on forever and a day. You never get rid of it, enemies that last for a lifetime.

DOC: What about things like visits, does that worry you?

MR: No, my father visits me once a week and that's all I get. I am quite happy with that. Other prisoners get their wives coming in to see them. They have got it very well set up. If I had a wife or a girlfriend or something come and visit me, or kids or that, I would be very happy because they have the best visitors' set-up in Pentridge in Jika Jika. In fact in a lot of ways Jika Jika is a wonderful division, it is just a . . .

DOC: So what is your daily routine?

MR: Well, my daily routine is different to the other daily routines. I sleep till about half-past nine, ten o'clock and get up and have a shower and I go down the yard and run around and I do a bit of exercise and I come up and have lunch and then I go to sleep till about four o'clock and then I get up, have tea, then I watch a bit of television, I come down for half an hour or an hour walk around, or a run around, and then I go back to sleep. I sleep a lot, like I am a bear hibernating.

DOC: How do you find it, do you find it boring or that time passes slowly?

MR: Well, I have trained myself not to think about whether something is boring or exciting; I just numb my mind to my surroundings, I couldn't really care less. I suppose other people could consider it boring. I don't even think about it. I guess it is boring, but it doesn't really worry me. I have been in situations like this for a long time, so you get used to it.

DOC: What do you think about H Division?

MR: It has always been the joke of the jail because you read the newspapers and you hear people talk about H Division, you imagine it is a very gruesome place, that you are bashed as soon as you arrive there, the prison officers tear your eyes out and eat 'em and all the rest of it, it really is a joke, the most violence in H Division is caused by other prisoners against each other, putting razor blades in the soap and poisoning the food, bashing each other, it is just a complete and utter joke. The only real trouble in H Division was caused by internal feuds. That is the only real danger in Pentridge.

DOC: How do you think the other prisoners would see you?

MR: They hate my guts, I am as popular as a pork chop in a synagogue because I don't agree with their theory on crime and their attitudes. I couldn't care less if they all lived and died. They are a bunch of completely gutless mugs, they stand in groups and attack with teams behind them and they come to jail for raping some sixty-two-year-old lady and they walk around the jail like a gangster. They don't like anyone who is indepen-dent, who wants to stand on their own, who wants to organise his own life and do his own thing and fight his own enemies on his own. They despise anyone trying to be an individual because they want everyone to conform to their standards. On one hand they hate society because society is trying to get them to conform to society's standards, yet they hate anyone in the underworld who tries to stand on their own two feet. You have got to be one of the boys. You have got to be one of the gang-sters and talk out of the side of the mouth.

DOC: How would you see the crimes that you committed?

MR: Every crime I have ever committed has been against a fellow criminal. So I don't think I've done anything of great seriousness. I don't think I've hurt anyone worth worrying about. So I can't see myself as having done anything very bad. Everyone I have ever shot or hurt or upset has never been anyone of great importance in my book. Just been a lot of whingers. Complainers who are gutless people. The jail's full of them. But I don't think they'd agree with my philosophies.

Gee, that was interesting reading after thirty years.

Margaret doesn't agree that Jika Jika was a better place for visitors than was H Division. But it was when it first opened, and probably for the first three years. Then they changed the H Division visiting area and made it better.

Margaret and I laughed out loud at that bit about not getting up until ten am and then having a sleep in the afternoon.

'Nothing's changed,' she said.

There's another observation I would make too when I think back on that time when Kevin Taylor cut off my ears – Quentin Tarantino doesn't know much about the subject. In *Reservoir Dogs*, Mr Blonde cuts off the copper's ear and there isn't much blood. I can tell you, when you cut off your ears, there is a lot of blood. A bloody lot of blood. And when your ears are on the ground after you've cut them off, they move around on their own. I likened it before to an Irish jig. So, I reckon that, as an expert on the cutting off of ears, Quentin Tarantino makes a good film director.

Cutting off my ears was not the first idea I had when I got told by the Classification Committee I would be in H Division forever. When I came back into the yard, I was reading a *National Geographic* and I saw an article on prostheses, artificial body parts. There was this bloke who had had his hand cut off and they had given him a hook, so I thought I would cut off my hand and get a hook to replace it. Some of the other prisoners said, 'Don't be stupid, Chopper, they will never let you have a hook in prison, you will have to wait until you get out if you want to do that.' And I guess I knew they were right, so that's when I got the idea to chop off my ears.

All up, looking at the DVD, my thinking hasn't really changed that much after thirty years.

I am not a complainer. I've never been a whinger. My mum tells a story about how I was sent off somewhere for a whole day once when I was a kid. When I came back, she asked me if I had had anything to eat.

My reply was, 'No, not a crumb.' I wasn't complaining, just telling the truth.

There were, though, a lot of whingers in Pentridge. But I just got on with it.

As I said before, around the time that documentary was made, the screws in H Division were getting a lot of bad press. But one of them, Peter Prideaux, came to my wedding and also to my fiftieth birthday party. So they can't all have been bad. A lot of them were, in fact, very helpful to me, or to Margaret.

As I mentioned earlier, when Peter Prideaux came to my fiftieth, it was the first birthday party I had ever had. We used to have Christmas parties in Pentridge. We got roast turkey, and the Salvation Army came in and played their instruments. And, of course, there was a famous Christmas party when we were supposed to have sausages.

While Jika Jika probably calmed down the Overcoat Gang War, it didn't completely end the madness. That's because there were a lot of mad people in Jika Jika.

I was the first one in, followed by a bloke by the name of Edwin John Eastwood, or Ted Eastwood. He had been found guilty of kidnapping a schoolteacher and six schoolchildren from a little town called Faraday in country Victoria in 1972. He demanded $1 million and the Victorian Government agreed to pay it. The premier, Sir Henry Bolte, sent the Minister for Education, Lindsay Thompson, up there with the money, but the kids and teacher got away before he had to hand it over. Ted Eastwood got fifteen years.

He escaped from Geelong Jail in 1976 and, a year later, took another schoolteacher and nine pupils hostage. This time, he wanted $7 million, guns, drugs and the release of a whole bunch of his mates at Pentridge. All he got was twenty-one years, with a minimum of eighteen.

He wrote a book about his life, too. It was called *Focus on Faraday and Beyond: Australia's Crime of the Century, the Inside Story*. That's probably bragging a bit, but as a crime, it was up there, all right, though, personally, I am opposed to any crime that puts women and children at risk. Eastwood's book earned some good reviews, especially from people who wanted to know what it was like to be in H Division and Jika Jika at about the same time as a bloke by the name of Chopper Read.

When I said I was mad in Jika Jika, it was because Ted Eastwood drove me mad. As well as foolishly thinking he could kidnap schoolteachers and get away with it, he had the ridiculous idea that he was a musician. He and his guitar just about drove me nuts. Thankfully, the last time he and I were teamed up in Jika Jika, the guitar went somewhere else – probably to J Ward because Ted had driven it mad, too – so we got on all right after that. He even wrote a note to go on the back of one of my books, *Chopper 2*.

Apparently, though, he wasn't all that happy about my description of his musical ability – or lack of it. He said, 'Do yourself a favour, Mark, and seek psychiatric help.'

My response was: 'I did go to the psychiatrist once, and when I went to leave, the doctor said, "Send in Ted Eastwood," ha ha.'

The third bloke into Jika Jika was Alex Tsakmakis. You've probably already guessed he was a Greek. He was also a millionaire businessman who had been convicted of murder.

We didn't get off to a good start in Jika Jika. Ted Eastwood had been taken away for a while, so it was just Alex and me in Jika Jika when one thing led to another, and I stabbed him in the neck with a pair of scissors.

Those scissors were an item of historical significance. They were probably the first to have found their way into Jika Jika and Tsakmakis claimed they were his. I disagreed, strongly.

There was blood everywhere. I wrote 'Sorry About That Alex' in his own blood on his cell door. As heartfelt as that apology was, it didn't do much for the friendship, but eventually we did become partners, united by that greatest of bonds – a mutual enemy.

Alex also taught me how to play chess. While moving the pieces around on the board, he would confide to me the details of some of his crimes.

Alex reckoned he'd killed a lot of people, or had had them killed. He told me he had killed this bloke from the National Gallery, curator Brian Finemore, just before he was supposed to take Princess Margaret on a guided tour of the place. Alex became known as the Barbecue King when he burned Barry Robert Quinn to death in Jika Jika.

I never thought much of Barry Robert Quinn. I have already gone on the public record as describing him as 'a coward, a liar, a junkie and a jail cat'. You can see I am undecided.

For those of you who don't know, a jail cat is someone who 'indulges in homosexual conduct behind prison walls'. Quinn had a long association with the Pentridge drag queen, Rhonda Rock Jaw. That was down in B Division.

I always thought that what Alex did to Barry Robert Quinn was a service to the community. He threw that glue that was used for making little model aeroplanes and cars all over Quinn and set fire to it.

Alex never made it out of Pentridge either. Craig 'Slim' Minogue whacked him in the head with a laundry bag full of gym weights. Smashed his skull to bits.

Minogue was called 'Slim' because he wasn't. He was about 150 kilos.

He also said he wasn't guilty of the Russell Street bombing. That was a bloody fiasco that cost a young policewoman her life. Craig 'Slim' Minogue would bore everyone with his insistence on his innocence. All up, five people were charged with the bombing and two were convicted, Craig Minogue and Stan Taylor.

The bomb went off on 27 March 1986, outside Russell Street police headquarters. The explosion smashed glass in buildings a block away. That's hardly surprising – there were about sixty sticks of gelignite inside a stolen car.

Angela Taylor was on her way to get lunch when the bomb went off. She was burned very badly and died twenty-four days afterwards. It seems she had tossed a coin with another copper, Dave Yeomans, about who would go and get their lunch. She lost the toss. She was the first Australian policewoman to die in the line of duty.

Another police officer, Carl Donadio, was thrown fifteen metres through the air and was also badly hurt by shrapnel, but lived. Altogether about twenty-one people were hurt.

To my way of thinking, just like the Walsh Street killings, the Russell Street bombing served no purpose at all except stupidity. The police don't go to water when you try to terrorise them. They come back stronger and tougher, and with the full force of the community and the government on their side.

When I was carrying out my psychological wars against the prisoners in H Division, I had a saying: you kill one and you scare 1000. But when you kill one copper, all you do is get another 1000 coppers hopping mad. And they can get away with a lot more, in the name of making the streets safe again for Mr and Mrs Citizen.

If the Russell Street bombers – and I know who they all were, not just the ones who got convicted – were going to set off a bomb, they should have given a ten-minute warning. That way, they could still have made their statement but the life of a young policewoman would not have been lost.

The Russell Street bombers have been described as having a pathological hatred of police. But the police officer they killed was hardly the type to be their sworn enemy. A few blokes at Pentridge reckoned they knew

Angela Taylor and that she was a very nice young lady. Apparently, she was working in the Melbourne City Watch House when Ted Eastwood's case was being heard, and part of her job was to feed the prisoners. As I said, hardly a sworn enemy.

Both Stan Taylor and Craig Minogue got life, with a non-parole period of thirty years. Craig Minogue's not due to be released until 2016. He has obtained a first-class honours degree while in prison and is now studying for a PhD. Not bad for a bloke who was illiterate when he first went inside. He's even got his own website. On it, he describes himself as a jailhouse lawyer, imprisoned educator and academic.

He certainly is the jailhouse lawyer. In the early days of his prison sentence, he was one of the people who rebelled against Jika Jika and the way prisoners were treated there. He did a real lot for prisoners' rights within Pentridge. He still occasionally takes the prison department to court, even now that Jika Jika is well and truly history.

Jika Jika stopped being part of Pentridge long before Pentridge itself was shut down to be turned into resi-dences. That's because, on 29 October 1987, prisoners erected a barricade inside Jika Jika in protest at their treatment. Someone set fire to the unit in which they had barricaded themselves. Five prisoners died and Jika Jika was shut down.

One of those prisoners was Jimmy Loughnan, the bloke who stabbed me in H Division. I was, of course, the one who gave Jimmy Loughnan the idea of setting fire to the unit to make a protest.

The other prisoners who died were Ricky Morris, Robert Wright, David McGauley and Arthur Gallagher.

Arthur Gallagher's mum used to talk to Margaret during visits and his mum was really looking forward to having him come home. He was due to be released in three months. He never made it.

As that other bloke who is buried in the grounds of Pentridge said: 'Such is life.'

CHAPTER 5

MEETING MARGARET IN PENTRIDGE

As you know, Margaret Cassar and I first bumped into each other in a fish and chip shop in Lalor when we were both teenagers. But we didn't meet properly until she began writing to me when I was in Pentridge for kidnapping the county court judge.

This is her story of how all that happened.

MARGARET: While Mark was serving the tail end of his nine-and-a-half-year sentence in September 1983, we met up and I visited Mark for the next four years. I have managed to keep all of his letters and they are neatly tucked away for Roy to read.

It all began one afternoon at work. One of my buddies there, Mary, asked me if I wanted to write to a guy in prison who her husband was serving time with.

I said I really didn't know if that would be the right thing for me to do, that I couldn't possibly go and visit a guy I didn't know. But Mary egged me on for a few days, telling me that most of the guys doing a long stretch hardly ever got outside mail or visits. Eventually, she talked me around.

I remember we both giggled behind our desks as we started to compose the letter together. The opening sentence began, 'Hi Mark, you must be wondering why one stranger would write to another stranger . . .'

The letters kept rolling in for some time before I even made it out to Pentridge for a visit. I actually got a flood of mail from Mark and it started to annoy me. I did say to Mary, 'This is really getting out of hand now and I will need to put a stop to it.'

I didn't want to continue writing and asked Mary whether the next time she went to visit her husband, Les, I could come too. I said I wanted to team up with her because I wanted to visit Mark in person to tell him I didn't want to write to him anymore. I didn't want to do that in a letter. Mary and I never managed to visit Pentridge at the same time, though.

A couple of weeks later, I found myself going on my own after Mark had booked a visit for me. It was a Sunday after-noon in September. Even though I was nervous, I could not wait to go. I wanted to tell him that all the letters had to stop, and that it was not possible for me to be going to prison to visit someone I didn't know.

When I got there, I was told I had to go to J Division. I had no idea what that meant, what category that was in the jail system. All I knew was that I had fallen into a pen-pal situation that I needed to get out of.

I was told that Mark would be along in five minutes but it turned out to be an unbelievably long five minutes. I remember thinking, 'If you don't hurry up, I will walk out.' My mind was really beginning to race – should I stay or should I go?

Then he walked out of the door and into the prison garden.

First impression: a solid, tall guy; a handsome brute.

Then he walked over to me and I realised he wasn't a complete stranger at all. He was the person I had seen in the fish and chip shop at Lalor all those years ago, when I was lining up for my piece of flake.

So, instead of being a parting of the ways, September 1983 was the start of a long friendship that has had its fair share of turmoil.

Eventually it led us to a beautiful wedding and a happy, certainly never boring, marriage.

When I reflect on that time and on where we are today, I can't help but feel that certain people are just meant to be together. Que sera sera, they were my mother's favourite words. Whatever will be, will be.

September is a very special month for Mark and me. It was also in September, in 2003, that our beautiful son, Roy, was born.

Roy really looks like his father did as a boy, and loves words and loves books. I am sure he will be just as witty and as imaginative.

But I am getting way ahead of myself.

Back in September 1983, Mark and I established a great friendship that turned into a romantic relationship. We had a solid understanding about that relationship. No promises were made to each other because you can't keep promises to someone while they are in prison. This is the downfall of a lot of relationships between inmates and their female visitors. The inmate expects the woman to be absolutely loyal to him and to love no other.

Back then, I had a very active and healthy social life and a great appetite for a good time. I wasn't going to let anyone interrupt that.

For his part, Mark did not stipulate any rules about whom I could see or where I could go. In fact, we wouldn't discuss this on our visits. It was all irrelevant to us as we enjoyed our little time together.

We were, and are, two realistic people. To this day, we do not stifle each other.

I went to see Mark each fortnight, on a pretty regular basis. From time to time, I would give myself a break, as the prison environment sometimes made the visits a bit tedious and regimental.

However, I still received plenty of phone calls – probably a few more than I should have but, hey, Mark was Mark. My regular visit was locked in at the same time each fortnight. I guess he had a few privileges and an advantage over the other guys. He was well liked by the prison officers and probably protected and favoured in a way.

When I visited, particularly towards the end of his sentence, our main focus was his release.

I have to say, looking back on all the complex issues we had to address, making sure everything was in accordance with the wishes of the Parole Board was both challenging and surprising.

But, as I have found out many times since, everything to do with Mark Read is a challenge and a surprise.

Anyway, even though the possible release date was getting nearer, that didn't mean he was just going to walk out of prison easily. From memory, Mark had three goes at applying to the Parole Board before he was successful. His colourful résumé let him down many times.

Being a model prisoner – yes, a model prisoner – he did come up for reclassification in Pentridge and was transferred to Bendigo Prison. This was apparently quite normal, I found out, to go to a medium-security prison to serve your remaining time.

As part of the Parole Board process, I had to obtain character references from reputable people for Mark. We had to convince the Parole Board that he was a changed man and was prepared to give the outside world his best shot. Our family solicitor, a friend of my mother's, who had known her when she was pregnant with me, wrote a beautiful and supportive letter. Mark's father wrote a letter, as did an old friend of Mark's who was a policeman who had known him as a teenager. He genuinely liked Mark. He knew the other side of him, the person he was before he went to Pentridge. He visited us many years later, when Mark came back to Melbourne from Tasmania, and said he was pleased that things had finally turned out for the best.

I forwarded these letters to the Parole Board. Then Mark told me to ring the board and have a chat to them. I was quite surprised by that request. I didn't think you could just ring up and talk to the Parole Board.

I somehow struck it lucky with the parole officer with whom I got to speak. His name was Mr Jim Jefferies and we sparked up a great rapport over the phone. He always made time for my calls and they were quite lengthy.

I don't imagine you could do that these days. From what I have been told, there was a much more personal feel back then, compared with now.

Mr Jefferies never steered me in the wrong direction. He reminded me many times of what Mark had to face with the Parole Board. Yet, I somehow could read between the lines and felt some confidence that Mark would be successful with his third request. After nine and a half years, he was finally going to be free.

And that's how it turned out. Mark fronted the board and his request for parole was granted.

When we were told he would be released, a friend of Mark's, Amos Atkinson, offered to drive me to Bendigo to pick him up. Amos, his wife and I travelled to Bendigo Prison. By one pm that day, Mark was a free man. For me, it was a great feeling finally to be taking him home. But, knowing what I know now, I realise that it must have been an horrendous experience for Mark.

When you have been locked away for nine and a half years, everything in your world is strange. Mark's mind was so severely conditioned to the confinement of Pentridge – to prison life amid some very hardened people. Unless you have experienced that, or are as close as Mark and I now are, the problems he was facing readjusting to life outside of prison are very hard to understand.

We eventually got back to Melbourne and arrived at our new place, and the new life we had talked about so much and had wanted for so long. I can honestly say now it was a tumultuous and testing time. It was certainly not what I thought it was going to be, but I guess I can say that it is where my real journey with Mark Read started.

I had chosen a place in Malvern, where I thought he would be happy. I didn't realise that the street I had picked had a tram line running down the middle of it. Mark had developed a real fondness for afternoon naps while he was in prison, and the rattle of the tram drove him mad, and not just during his naps. The last tram would go past at one am and they would start again at four am. Mark said he was always dreaming about trams.

So, he got permission from the Parole Board to go and live with his father in Tasmania, near Launceston. I then went back to my house in Collingwood.

The rest of that time is discussed elsewhere in this book, a time that eventually led to Mark going back to prison for arson and shooting Chris Liapis.

Fortunately for Mark, being an old resident of Pentridge, he was comfortable with going back. In fact, he felt relieved, something I now understand. The outside world wasn't kind to him, especially when there was no real preparation for his release. He had no money, and no means of making any. As I said, this process was a real eye-opener for me. I realised that there were no real support services for ex-prisoners. There certainly wasn't any real support for us as a couple.

We had great intentions, there's no doubt about that. But all Mark got from 'the system' was his release date, some adverse publicity and 'See you later'. The rest was up to us. So, I now understand why so many ex-prisoners end up back in jail.

I know there is a lot of research being done that will hopefully lead to the better reintegration of prisoners into the community. A woman called Dr Lesley Hardcastle, from Deakin University, is studying this.

Dr Hardcastle believes there are many benefits from the successful reintegration of prisoners into the community. In an article I read on the Deakin University website, she said:

As well as the social reasons, there's the economic argument.

It costs more than $80,000 a year to keep an offender in prison.

With a community-based corrections order, it is less than $10,000.

It is really important to learn what it is we can do in terms of corrections programs to prepare people to return to the community.

I think it is important for the community to know what it can do to help with the re-integration process.

Unfortunately, stereotyping of offenders makes community acceptance difficult. When a person gets out on parole and commits another serious offence, it's on the front page. But you never read about the people who successfully re-integrate.

Not every offender is a danger to the community. Some have just been unlucky and want to get on with their lives once they have served their sentence.

That requires a lot of support from the community. They need an employer to give them a job, and the willingness of other people to accept them in their neighbourhood.

Many people may say that they believe that re-integration of ex-offenders is good, as long as it's not in their community.

If through this project we can develop some models

for successful re-integration, then we can go to the community with more confidence to say that this works and that's got to have a whole range of benefits for everyone, including the taxpayer.

Mark did have a great home to come to but because he had been so scarred by prison, this still wasn't enough for us to live a normal life together. While he was in jail, he had always been heavily medicated. The Xanax and injections, and so on, were supposed to make him into a zombie, yet he was still hyperactive. In my opinion, the things he was prescribed only worsened his violent mental state. We have now discovered his condition was incorrectly diagnosed and he was prescribed the wrong medication.

And that really worries me, when I know how many prisoners are heavily medicated while in jail. How on earth was Mark supposed to function normally?

Of course, prison, and especially Pentridge back then, is a long way from normal. You only need to look at the prison yard in *Chopper*, the movie, to know that. It was an isolated area of the prison used as a yard. There was no grass; there were no windows to look out from. It had a closed roof so you couldn't even see the blue sky above you. There was no fresh air. The guys just stayed out there for hours and hours, pacing like tigers. No wonder so much violence was able to brew in that yard.

When Mark was released, he was given his medication that morning. That was it; there was no advice on where to get future medication. I was never even told that he needed medical attention, and nor was the Parole Board. He was severely addicted to his medication, so that without it, he would have withdrawal symptoms – violent withdrawal symptoms. That was a recipe for disaster, and disaster was what we got.

Fortunately for me, the unusual connection Mark had with the prison officers extended to his time out of jail.

Four prison officers were great to us: Colin Frost, Graham Hartley, Peter Prideaux and Tim McEwan, all of whom have now gone elsewhere. In actual fact, all the prison officers of H Division were just fantastic, as far as their treatment of me was concerned. I was brought up to treat people as you find them and that is exactly what I did. Jail can make or break a relationship, and without the extra support I received from those officers, I am sure my relationship with Mark would have ended a long time ago.

I am so glad it didn't, that somehow we were able to persevere until we could find a way to give Mark the life skills he needed, proper medical treatment and, ultimately, the life we dreamed of when he first came out of jail in 1986.

Phew!

As Margaret was writing this, the news came through that the policeman, Garry Schipper, who had written that reference for me had passed away.

I had known him since I was fourteen years old. I met him when I was working part-time for a furniture removal company. He was working there part-time too, as well as holding down a full-time job as a police officer. He was a giant of a man: six foot five and almost 160 kilos back then. He was the driver of the furniture van and I was the jockey. We'd spend all day together shifting furniture.

I met him again years later, when I first got arrested for assaulting three police officers. That was at the Ringwood police station.

Garry Schipper was also a sailor. He was a member of the Sandringham Yacht Club. He used to crew on the boats of very wealthy people, like Lou Abrahams, who enter the Sydney to Hobart race every year. He was a member of Lou Abraham's crew on *Ultimate Challenge*, when it won the race on handicap in 1989.

In 1998, in the wee small hours of the morning, during the Sydney to Hobart race, he was washed overboard when his boat was hit by a huge wave. He'd been up on deck checking the sails and so on. He wasn't wearing a life jacket; all that he was holding onto when he went into the water was a Dolphin torch. He was bouncing around in Bass Strait for about twenty hours, flicking the light on and off until he got rescued. After that, he got a job advertising Dolphin torches. In the advertisement, he would say, 'If it wasn't for the Dolphin torch, I wouldn't be here today.' He told Margaret and me the same thing when he came to visit us in Collingwood.

Garry also became a very strong advocate of safety for sailors. He would go to conferences, and tell the story about the torch and tell everyone to wear an inflatable life jacket.

When he retired from the police force, he was a chief inspector. I remember that the day he came to see us in Collingwood, he was in full uniform. It was a surprise visit. He said he just wanted to catch up and also to apologise for not coming to our wedding.

Garry Schipper was a really good bloke and a really good policeman. I know he got caught up in the Beach inquiry into police corruption at one stage, but was cleared of any wrongdoing. He was supposed to have pushed a bloke by the name of Stephen Sellers down the stairs at the Prahran police station.

I didn't have a high opinion of Stephen Sellers, so I would have taken Garry Schipper's word on the matter if I was listening to the evidence. I once tried to drown Sellers in a bubble bath in a massage parlour. I nearly succeeded, but two ladies gave him mouth-to-mouth and saved him, only for him to run his car off the road some time later. He hit a gum tree near Orbost.

I think the Beach inquiry was also investigating Garry Schipper for holding prisoners by their ankles out of the armed robbery squad windows. He was strong enough to do that. He could pick up a huge Westinghouse fridge, and lift it off the back of the furniture truck on his own.

Garry was in the armed robbery squad at the time of the Great Bookie Robbery in 1976. As I have already said, no one got convicted for that crime and most of the money was never recovered.

But all this is no longer of concern to Garry Schipper, a dear friend.

Thanks for that friendship, Garry, and for helping me get out of Pentridge back in 1986. I just wish I had been able to stay out a bit longer.

CHAPTER 6

THE SHOOTING OF SAMMY THE TURK

I did some truly mad things during the seven months I was out of prison in 1987. I never involved Margaret in my activities, though, or even discussed them with her.

I was living in Malvern and really struggling to cope with a lot of things. One of them was the sound of the trams; the squeak of their wheels on the tracks. It drove me nuts. I was used to the peace and quiet of Pentridge. As I've said, in H Division, if anyone made a noise after lockdown they got two weeks added to their sentence.

I asked my parole officer if I could move to Ravenswood in Tasmania, where my dad was living. I had to get permission from the Parole Board, and I fronted Justice Alastair Borthwick Nicholson, the Chief Justice of the

Victorian Supreme Court and the head of the Parole Board, with a .32 calibre hand gun under my coat.

I didn't realise I had the gun until I was walking out of the hearing, and thought to myself, 'Thank God they didn't search me.' If they had searched me and found the weapon, it would have been straight back into prison for me, especially as I'd fronted up to a Supreme Court judge with it on. I had just got out of prison for trying to abduct a county court judge with a gun; no one was going to believe that I had just forgotten I had a gun on me when I turned up to put my case to Justice Nicholson. It was just another sign of how mad everything was at that time, after I'd been spending so much time in prison.

Fortunately, they never found out about the gun and I got permission to live in Tasmania. I would go down on Monday and come back Friday, and have the weekends in Melbourne, where I got up to a lot of no good.

A lot of people were making money out of drugs, an enterprise that had been building up nicely in Melbourne while I was in Pentridge doing my nine and a half years. As I've already said, I reckon the time of the Great Bookie Robbery, in 1976, was the end of the good old days of Australian crime, as, after that, drugs came into the industry and ruined it. I guess that, by the time I got out, in November 1986, I was pretty sure some of these drug dealers wouldn't mind sharing just a bit of their proceeds with me.

Shortly after my release in 1986, I also started hanging out with three officers from the armed robbery squad. A prison officer I'd become friendly with while in

Bendigo Prison had introduced me to them, and assured me they were all 'on the level'. They used to take me out for counter lunches, and would drive me all over Melbourne, wherever I wanted to go. I was using them as a taxi service and later they told the Supreme Court they were using me as an informant.

They didn't need, nor did they get, any information from me. The truth was, I was the one needing information from them on who it was who had a contract, or contracts, on my head. There were a lot of rumours that a lot of people wanted me dead. I started wearing a bulletproof vest everywhere I went.

It was not until recently that I fully realised how much these coppers were leading me up the garden path. They were trying to start a gangland war between me and people like Alphonse Gangitano, Mushie Farrell, Shane Goodfellow, Graeme Jensen and Jason Moran. They were trying to stir up the same kind of hatred that existed more recently between the late Jason Moran and the now equally late Carl Williams, and that led to that lot of gangland killings in Melbourne. Maybe they saw this as a way of cleaning up the Melbourne criminal element – getting rid of Chopper Read, Alphonse Gangitano and so on.

Also, these police officers worked closely with some well-connected journalists. Margaret believes none of us knew we were 'at war' until we started reading sensational newspaper stories. Once these police told me there was a contract on my head, I just had to know who was behind it and why. I was out night and day trying to find out the truth. But no one seemed to know.

I had a screaming argument with Amos Atkinson, one of the members of the Overcoat Gang in Pentridge, but he couldn't tell me who was behind it. There was just a lot of madness and, I guess, a lot of paranoia around. And all this eventually led to the death of Sammy the Turk in the early hours of the morning.

I went to Footscray to see Shane Goodfellow because I had been told by these three police he was one of the blokes putting up money for a contract to have me shot. Now, Shane and I had a bit of history, going right back to my first days in Pentridge. I had bashed him up in 1979, so it was understandable that he might be the one wanting me killed.

I turned up at Shane's place and he said he wouldn't let me in unless I put all my guns through the door first. So I handed over a magnum colt, a .410 sawn-off shotgun, a stick of gelignite, a .32 calibre hand gun and a .22 calibre rifle, but I kept a .32 calibre Beretta down the front of my pants. By 1987, gelignite had become another of my tricks of the trade. I would tape it to the outside of my body, and walk into a place and threaten to detonate it unless certain moneys were handed over. Why did I wear it on the outside of my clothes? Well, no one could see it if I wore it under them, could they, and they mightn't take me seriously.

After I handed over the guns, I heard Shane Good-fellow going off about the .410 sawn-off shotgun, laughing and saying that it was a lady's gun. So, when I got inside, I pulled out the Beretta and put it to Shane Goodfellow's head and told him that the .410 sawn-off shotgun could still do a good job of killing someone.

His wife, Kim Powell, came in and threw a full nappy at me. I don't know if you've ever had a poo-filled nappy thrown at you but it really puts you off.

Kim said, 'Shane doesn't want to kill you, Chopper; why would he want to kill you? And you don't want to kill him then.'

That must have made sense to me. I then took the gun away from Shane Goodfellow's head.

I looked around me and saw the way Shane was living and it wasn't all that flash. He might have been an enemy of mine, but I had admired him for his tough-ness. Bloody drugs, though, they had taken away his toughness. He was a mess.

I gave him $1000 and said, 'Fix yourself up, Shane; you shouldn't be living like this.'

Not that long ago, one of Shane Goodfellow's sons turned up at my home. Shane had two sons, Shane Junior and Jimmy. When I visited, Kim was pregnant with Jimmy, so it was probably Shane Junior's pooey nappy that she threw at me. And it was Shane Junior who came to my house in Collingwood and he did look like his father, I have to say.

I asked him why he had come and he said, 'I have every right to come here; I want to get some answers about my father.' He then started crying and I put my arm around him. I told him to go and talk to his mother about his father.

Anyway, back to the night that Sammy the Turk died. After Kim Powell had convinced me not to kill Shane Goodfellow, I told them I was going to go to Bojangles nightclub to try to find out just who it was who was trying to have me killed. Well, Goodfellow must have rung all the other blokes who were supposed to be trying to get me killed: Alphonse, Mushie Farrell, Jason Moran, Graeme Jensen, and so on, and they'd all met up at Shane's place and headed down to Bojangles too. I reckon they had by then decided they were going to kill me.

There were two car parks at Bojangles nightclub, a brightly lit one and a dark one. Kim Powell had gone into the nightclub and talked Sammy the Turk into taking me outside, on the pretext of selling me a hand gun.

He walked out into the dark car park. I guess he thought that if anyone was going to kill anyone, they would do it in the dark car park, not the brightly lit one. So, he lured me into the dark car park, a move that cost him his life.

This is the story I told the homicide squad, this is the story I told the Supreme Court jury and this is the story I am telling you now.

Sammy the Turk said, 'You got gun, you got gun.'

I said, 'Yeah,' and lifted the front of my jacket and showed him the Beretta. I stuck a bullet in the chamber and let the hammer back down. To make it discharge, you have to pull the hammer back and then pull the trigger.

He then started pulling the gun's trigger. He went click, click, click and was trying to shoot me. But the gun didn't go off because he didn't know you had to pull the hammer back first. I then pulled out the .410 sawn-off shotgun and shot him through the eyeball.

He was dead before he hit the ground.

I could hear Kim Powell screaming and crying, and then she ran off and hopped into a car. I heard a car driving off from the well-lit car park.

I saw all the blokes, Shane, Alphonse, Jason, Mushie and so on, screaming away in a car. I hadn't realised until then that they were all there to kill me, but had been waiting in the brightly lit car park. Why would you kill someone in a brightly lit car park when you could do it in a dark one?

Amateurs!

I walked past the bouncer and said, 'Did you see what happened? Then you'd better forget about it pretty quickly.'

I said to the manager of Bojangles, 'I just shot a Turk out the front.'

I went up to Gonzo Gazetti, a member of the Painters and Dockers who I knew, and he said, 'I think you should go home now, Chopper.'

As I walked out, I opened the gun and threw a shell up on the roof of the nightclub and then took a taxi home. I put the .32 Beretta behind a pot plant at my brother-in-law's house. He lived across the road in Collingwood.

Later that day, at the Fawkner Club Hotel, I met up with my three mates from the armed robbery squad, I reckon it was about six-thirty pm.

I said to them, 'I have just shot that Turk this morning.'

They told me the homicide squad had already arrested someone else for the murder. Apparently, Sammy the Turk had had a fight with a young bloke a couple of days before. The homicide squad believed he had returned to back up his fight with a .410 shotgun. When I said I had done it, the blokes from the armed robbery squad thought I was trying to trick them. It wasn't until a couple of weeks later that they arrested me for murder.

Alphonse and I didn't like each other much, but I don't think either of us really wanted to kill the other. After all, I was the first bloke to give Alphonse a gun – a beaut little sawn-off shotgun. Mad Charlie had said to me once, 'You know Alphonse, he hasn't got a gun.' My father had made this nice little sawn-off shotgun for me and I gave it to Alphonse.

He even wanted me to join his gang in Carlton.

I said, 'I can't join your gang, Alphonse, it would mean sitting around in Johnny's Green Room, wearing a suit.'

Johnny's Green Room was a place they used to hang around in Faraday Street, Carlton, next to Brunetti.

I called all of the Carlton Crew the Plastic God-fathers. Once, in 1976, when I had just got out of jail, I bumped into Alphonse and a few of his mates in the Dover Hotel. They were happy to see me at that moment, I think.

Well, they made out they were.

I went to the toilet to have a poo and the next thing I knew, they kicked the door open, and were in the toilet, punching the shit out of me – while I was trying to have a poo.

I closed my eyes and started punching back, and when I opened my eyes again, Alphonse had gone, I was just fighting the bouncers. I shot the place up the next night.

I never did see Alphonse again.

When he did get killed, on 16 January 1998, aged forty, his death sparked a lot of gangland killings. I got questioned about his murder, even though I had nothing to do with it. I got questioned because just before I got out of Risdon Prison, a reporter, Rochelle Jackson from Channel 7, had come to visit me. She asked me if I was prepared to appear on television with Alphonse Gangitano once I got out. She asked me this about six or seven weeks prior to his death. I said to her that I didn't think Alphonse would be alive by the time I got out. I wasn't due to be released until six or eight weeks after Alphonse was killed. When my prediction came true, the police wanted to find out what I knew about Alphonse's death.

At the same time, Jason Moran started a whispering campaign that I had something to do with it.

Yeah, while I was in prison in Hobart. You'd need a bloody big gun to shoot someone in Templestowe, Victoria, from there. Of course, that bit of logic didn't stop Jason Moran. He was putting out a story that there was already a headstone with my name on it.

I made my prediction to Rochelle Jackson, not because I was involved in Alphonse Gangitano's death but because I knew what Big Al had been up to. He had fallen out with Jason Moran over an incident at the Sports Bar in King Street, Melbourne, in 1995. Big Al, Jason and Troy Rapasarda were charged with some serious assaults on a number of patrons. Al had virtually given Jason up over the incident, which Jason was pleading not guilty to.

I also knew about a bashing at an Italian wedding, during which Al had splattered blood over the bride and groom. He had made his offence even worse by not offering to apologise. I also knew the name of the person he had bashed at this wedding and that the person's family was very prominent and well respected. If I had even accidentally bumped into a member of this family, let alone bashed a member of it and left him or her splattered with their own blood, I would have been apologising pretty quickly.

The reason for Gangitano bashing a member of a prominent Italian family was pretty silly. Apparently, the family had come into a lot of money after selling a business and Al thought he was entitled to some of it, I don't know why. One night when Alphonse was at the casino, he sent some underlings to see a young Italian man. The underlings said that if the gentleman in question could see his way fit to lend Alphonse Gangitano around $10,000 or $20,000, as a matter of some urgency, the hand of friendship would always be there. The young Italian sent his apologies to Alphonse Gangitano, saying he couldn't lend him the money.

And no more was said on the matter until some months later, when both Alphonse and the young Italian gentleman ended up at this wedding involving two very prominent Italian families – on the bride's side and on the groom's. These families were well known and very respected around Melbourne's markets.

Alphonse Gangitano's refusal to offer on the spot both families his heartfelt apologies for bashing someone and splattering the bride and groom with blood meant that he had about a month to put things right. That's what usually happens – you have a month to put something right or you go on the missing persons list. I based my prediction to Rochelle Jackson on all this.

I had mixed with Italians in Thomastown when I was growing up, and knew how they worked. Italians are very predictable people. If racehorses and jockeys were all Italians, I reckon I could tip a winner seven times out of ten.

The facts are that Alphonse was last seen in the company of Graham Kinniburgh and Jason Moran. At the coroner's inquest into Alphonse's death, they were exempt from giving evidence, on the grounds it might incriminate them. That's a bit like saying 'No comment' to the media.

I was happy to give evidence when I was charged with the murder of Sammy the Turk, and I eventually got off. Colin Lovitt, my barrister, was magnificent. Shortly after my hearing, he was made a Queen's Counsel. In my humble view, he well and truly deserved it. Colin Lovitt has made a career out of defending people charged with murder. His belief is, no matter how notorious the crime or how incriminating the evidence, everyone is entitled to a fair trial.

The way he dismissed the forensic evidence against me was brilliant.

He said to the judge and the jury, 'What can you say about forensic evidence?

'May I remind Your Honour and members of the jury of the case of Lindy Chamberlain and the blood in the car?'

Lindy Chamberlain was, of course, charged with the murder of her little baby, Azaria. A forensic scientist claimed that blood was found in the Chamberlains' Torana and that it was the sort of blood that could only come from a tiny baby – foetal haemoglobin. What it really was was Dufix, which got sprayed into a lot of Toranas. Apparently, it was used to deaden road noise. So, forensic science was getting a bit of a bad press at the time.

When Sammy the Turk got shot, there was no dingo around to blame. It was me who shot him but Colin Lovitt was arguing strenuously that it was done in self-defence. Knocking the forensic evidence for six was a good start.

We also had a newly appointed judge, Justice McDonald, who was presiding over his first murder trial. That played into our hands a bit too.

One way Colin Lovitt works is to pick a fight with judges and get them angry with him. He made Justice McDonald angry with him.

You had a barrister correcting a judge on a point of law and the judge getting quite upset, then apologising, and Colin Lovitt then apologising to him. He is a very clever lawyer, Colin Lovitt; I don't think he has ever lost a murder case.

When he finished his final address on my behalf, the jury went out for the day. They came back at a quarter to nine at night.

I remember walking, under a full moon, across the bluestone courtyard from the old Supreme Court cells. There I was, going to hear a verdict on whether I was guilty of murder and up in the sky was this full moon shining down on me. It was surreal.

I remember that Little Peter Allen was also in the Supreme Court cells that night. We were supposed to be enemies because, as I said, I had bashed his brother Dennis in Pentridge.

As I walked past him, I said, 'My jury's back.'

He said, 'Good luck, Chopper,' and he meant it. Even your enemies wish you good luck when you're facing a murder charge.

I went back to court number four. The jury walked in and the judge asked the foreman for the verdict. 'Not guilty.'

It was amazing.

I walked back across the bluestone courtyard under the moonlight and it was even more surreal. Then I got back to H Division, walked in the door and yelled, 'NOT GUILTY!' and the whole prison cheered.

A couple of weeks later, I was back in court for sentencing, after pleading guilty to burning down Nick the Greek's house in Footscray and for shooting Chris Liapis. I just didn't like Nick, so I burned his house down. It was much the same with Chris Liapis; he was a loudmouth. On top of that, they were both drug dealers.

Whenever I've been asked why I burned Nick's house down, my reply has been, 'I love a sunburned country.'

For a while after I set fire to his house, I would send Nick Apostolidis a Christmas card that read (apologies to Jerry Lee Lewis):

I shook your walls and I rattled your brain.

My kind of love just drove you insane.

I broke your will.

Oh what a thrill.

Goodness gracious, great balls of fire.

Ha ha.

I shot Chris Liapis in the guts. I then told him, 'Justice comes out of the end of a barrel.' He knew I didn't mean a beer barrel.

It was about this time that I developed a great affection for members of the Albanian community in Melbourne. After I shot Liapis, Neville Dardovski took me back to his family's hotel, the Builders Arms, in Gertrude Street, Fitzroy, and I stayed the night there.

Neville's father was a wonderful old man by the name of Norm Dardovski; a gentleman of the old school who believed in an eye for an eye. I am very grateful to the Dardovskis because they probably saved my life a few times back in the 1980s. Their two hotels were real safe havens for me – a bit like Fort Knox.

A lot of people think that Neville Bartos in the movie *Chopper* is based on Neville Dardovski. I could never have shot Neville in the leg and lived to tell the tale. But Neville the Albanian has become pretty famous, courtesy of *Chopper*.

I am also very grateful to another member of my defence team, Pat Harvey, a legal aid solicitor. It was said that if you got Pat Harvey as your legal aid solicitor, you would always get a good barrister like Colin Lovitt. I spent a lot of time with Pat and was always impressed by his thoroughness and compassion. He has a real feel for helping crims.

I think he wanted to help me because he liked my sense of humour. I had a well-deserved reputation around the courts for being an entertaining witness. I could have judges and juries, even police and prosecutors, in fits of laughter with my razor-sharp wit.

Pat Harvey also got me another good barrister, Boris Kayser, for when I pleaded guilty to arson and shooting Chris Liapis. I got two years for each offence and was pretty happy about that. Four years was a lot better than a life sentence for murder.

I think my father was happy too, not so much about the length of the sentence, but because I was back in prison. He used to say that at least in prison I'd get three meals a day. And I'd have to say that, after all the madness and paranoia of the time I was out in 1987, there was something reassuring about going back into Pentridge. At least I couldn't hear the bloody trams when I was trying to get to sleep.

After what these three members of the armed robbery squad did to me, telling me all that bullshit, people might wonder how I feel about the police now. I have got nothing against police; I don't distrust or trust them, I am ambivalent towards them.

One of the things I've always said is that there is not a lot of difference between the world of the policeman and the world of the professional criminal. A policeman has to learn to think like a professional criminal. A professional criminal has to learn to think like a policeman. The problems arise when they start thinking like the other person too well. That's when police become standover merchants in their own right, as happened on the Golden Mile in Kings Cross – and a few other places. And God help us all when criminals start thinking too much like police.

Next, crims will start thinking they can write books.

CHAPTER 7

MARK READ, THE AUTHOR

I became an author while serving those four years in Pentridge for burning down Nick the Greek's house (and his drugs) and shooting Chris Liapis.

My first book, *Chopper from the Inside*, was published in December 1991. This is my fourteenth book.

Amazing, isn't it, how a bloke who couldn't get past Form Two in high school has become a best-selling author, with more than 500,000 books sold all over the world, and probably twice that, if the truth be known. And they're not just best-sellers, but critically acclaimed best-sellers, as you will see soon.

It all started in 1990, when a journalist by the name of John Silvester came to see me in H Division. He was working for a Melbourne newspaper called *The Sun Pictorial*. It has since amalgamated with *The Herald* to become *The Herald Sun*.

The first time he wrote about me, he really bagged me. I sent him a letter that said my idea of happiness would be for a 1000-room hotel to burn down and for a journalist from *The Herald Sun* to be found dead behind the door of every room.

I kept writing, and he came back and saw me again. I gave him a whole article that I had written on foolscap paper while I was in my cell. John took it away and reproduced the whole thing in *The Herald Sun*, and got his front page, and two or three other pages inside the paper. It was my words but it had his name on it.

I thought, 'This is pretty good, I can write well enough to get published in the newspaper even if my name isn't on it.'

So I wrote to him again and said, 'Why don't we write a book?'

And he said, 'No, you write a book, Chopper. You write out some good stories and send them to me, and if I think you've got enough good stories – well, don't worry, I will get them published.'

So, I started writing out these stories: big, heavy stories about my life in Pentridge and the things that had got me there. I would write on both sides of the foolscap paper and number the pages on the top. When I had ten foolscap sheets, I had twenty pages of writing, and I would mail them to Margaret and she would send them to John Silvester.

Pretty soon, John Silvester had received about 120 pages and he said, 'I think we've got enough for a book.'

I sent him about sixty more pages and forty pictures, and he and his friend Andrew Rule, another journalist who writes about the crime scene in Melbourne, published this book called *Chopper from the Inside*. It wasn't all that well printed and put together, this first book, and all the pages fell out. But we've fixed that since then.

That first book has now been reprinted thirty-six times. That would almost put it up there with the Bible. On the cover of the latest edition was a little line that said that more than 200,000 copies had been sold and stolen around the world. Apparently, my books are also very popular with shoplifters.

Back in December 1991, when the first copies were printed, everything was about doing it on the cheap. I only got a dollar a book and I still only get a dollar a book. There was a lot of hoo-ha at the time about me living on the proceeds of crime, but the same could be said of Andrew Rule and John Silvester.

And plenty of others.

Also, a lot of other people who write so-called true crime books don't know anything about the subject.

As I wrote in the foreword to *Chopper from the Inside*:

Without any disrespect to police, the NCA (the National Crime Authority that was set up following the Costigan Royal Commission), and investigative journalists, they all stand on the outside straining their eyes to look inside the criminal world ... The truth is, the underworld is a cess pit, not a science.

So, why wouldn't you get an expert from the underworld to write books on true crime? And it's better than me living off the dole, off the Australian taxpayer.

I've said before that, if you get out of jail and make a living cleaning out the toilets for the local council, they call it rehabilitation and say how wonderful it is. But they don't like you climbing too high up the social ladder. So, if you become a best-selling author, you get accused of living off the proceeds of crime.

Andrew Rule and John Silvester – or Sly and Greedy, as I jokingly call them – have done pretty well out of the books. Andrew lives in Caulfield and John has a beautiful double-storey home in Blackburn. As well as making them plenty of money, Chopper Read has saved Andrew Rule and John Silvester a lot of money, too.

In 2005, they were being sued for defamation by Abe Saffron, the gentleman from Sydney who was known as Mr Sin. Saffron was famous for suing for defamation and he won most times. He had John and Andrew on toast because they had called him a criminal in print, in their book *Tough: 101 Australian Gangsters*. Abraham Gilbert Saffron's only major conviction was for tax evasion.

In desperation, they came to me and asked if I knew 'anyone who can reach out to Abe Saffron and pull his coat'. Even though I didn't know Abe Saffron from a bar of soap, I said I could do that.

At that stage, I had been working the public-speaking circuit with Roger Rogerson, the former New South Wales detective. I knew he knew Abe Saffron quite well. I asked Roger to tell Abe that he would be doing me a personal favour if he dropped the case, as these two blokes were my personal publishers.

Rogerson went and spoke to Saffron. It seems Abe Saffron said that, 'If these blokes are the personal publishers of Chopper Read, I will do that as a personal favour to him.' The day after Abe said that, the case was dropped. I saved them a million bucks.

Abe Saffron, I later discovered, thought quite highly of me. His son, Alan, mentioned me favourably in the book he wrote about his father, *Gentle Satan: My Life with Abe Saffron*. It came out in 2008, a couple of years after Abe's death.

I don't know how many copies Abe Saffron's son's book sold, but I know my first book did pretty well. So, John and Andrew kept coming back for more. And I just kept writing more books.

You'd buy them for the clever titles alone.

Chopper 2 – Hits and Memories. Detective Sergeant Rob Wilson wrote a small critique on the back: 'Mark Brandon Read has done for literature what Hannibal Lecter did for vegetarianism.'

Chopper 3 – How to Shoot Friends and Influence People. I read a lot of Dale Carnegie's works when I was in Pentridge, then came up with my own ideas on the matter.

Chopper 4 – For the Term of his Unnatural Life. This was the book that they tried to ban. I was told by the governor of Risdon Prison I couldn't send letters to John Silvester and Andrew Rule anymore because it appeared I was trying to write another book. I had to pay my legal bills somehow, didn't I?

Chopper 5 – Pulp Faction. My first foray into writing crime fiction. Get out of the way, Patricia Cornwell.

Chopper 6 – No Tears for a Tough Guy. My second foray into writing crime fiction. The names have been changed to protect – well, everyone, really, guilty and innocent.

Chopper 7 – The Singing Defective. I liked the little quotes on the back of this one:

'. . . written with verve and pace, and has the ring of authenticity' – Professor HP Helseltine, Miles Franklin Literary Award Judge

'What's verve mean?' – Mark Brandon Read

Chopper 8 – The Sicilian Defence. I really liked the comments in the 'About the Author' section in this book: 'Read has appeared on national television, though he has no recollection of this. He has an extensive CV, an expensive QC, recorded a CD and has ingested substantial amounts of VB.'

Chopper 9 – The Final Cut. Probably the best line in this book was the caption below a photo of my son Charlie and me: 'I have learned that babies are like drug dealers, they cry a lot and shit themselves.'

Chopper 10½ – The Popcorn Gangster. This is the book that upset Judy Moran. It's one of my favourites for that alone.

Chopper 11 – Last Man Standing – From Ex-Con to Icon.

Some of these books were fact, some were fiction, some were faction. None of them got pulped. They were all best-sellers.

And, whatever else they were, they were good enough to get me admitted to the Australian Society of Authors. I have the certificate, signed by Anne Deveson AO.

All up, my ventures into the genre of true crime have sold squillions and my name's up there in lights with some of the most famous authors in the bloody world. If you go to one of those online places to buy books, they have a section that says, 'People who bought this book also bought books by these authors.' And have a look at some of the names that come up for my titles:

Hunter S Thompson
Lenny McLean
Charles Bronson (yeah, *the* Charles Bronson)
Cormac McCarthy
Philip Carlo
Roberto Saviano
Ralph Steadman

Literary giants, all of them – well, apart from Charles Bronson, perhaps – and Chopper Read's name is up there with theirs.

And how about some of the reviews over the years?

'An Australian folk hero,' said *The New York Times*. Eat your heart out, Banjo Paterson and the Man from Snowy River.

'The tale of a brute and a braggart,' said *The New Yorker* of my first book. Well, up yours.

'Read is a publicity stunt on hairy legs,' said *Newsday*. And?

Then I got into writing these adult fairytales.

They caused a bit of a stir, too, especially *Hooky the Cripple*, which was illustrated by my friend, Archibald Prize–winning painter Adam Cullen.

People claimed *Hooky the Cripple* was politically incorrect. Well, that would have had to have been the first time that 'politically correct' and 'Mark Read' ever got said in the same sentence. Brendan Nelson, the politician, went ballistic when it was suggested *Hooky the Cripple* might become a Queensland textbook.

Hooky the Cripple was based on a story that my dad told me. Hooky kills a butcher who has badly mistreated him over a very long period of time. He is saved from the death sentence by Giovanno from Milano. I named him after the man I met in the mental hospital.

At Hooky's court hearing no one will defend him. There are 2000 people in the courtroom, including the judge, the king, the pope, and the greatest prosecutor in Italy.

The judge yells, 'Will anyone defend this criminal?'

The door opens and a little man with a walking stick comes in. They all go 'Aaaaaah!'

Standing in the doorway is Giovanno from Milano, the greatest lawyer in Italy, who has never lost a case in sixty years.

The judge says, 'The court is honoured to have you here.'

Giovanno sits down and says he will defend the cripple.

The first witness is called, and is questioned by the best prosecutor in Italy. The witness talks about how the butcher was a kind man and Hooky was a murdering beast, and that the butcher did nothing to upset the cripple. He didn't spit on him, or kick him or beat him; this evidence, of course, was completely untrue.

At the end of the first witness's evidence, the judge asks Hooky's lawyer if he wants to say anything.

The lawyer gets up and says, 'My name is Giovanno from Milano and I bring you greetings.'

Then he sits down.

Another witness is called and gives his evidence.

When the judge asks Giovanno from Milano if he has anything to say, he answers, 'I am Giovanno from Milano and I bring you greetings.'

Witness after witness, he just keeps repeating this. After about ten days, all the people in the court, the king, the pope and the judge, are getting sick of it.

The judge says, 'Thank you for your greeting but do you have anything else to say?'

Giovanno from Milano just says, 'My name is Giovanno from Milano and I bring you greetings.'

By now the judge is starting to lose it. 'What have you got to say, Giovanno?' he yells.

And Giovanno just repeats it again.

The judge picks up a gavel, throws it down from the bench and hits Giovanno on the head. The judge leaps over the dock and starts to strangle Giovanno.

The police have to drag the judge off and he keeps shouting, 'Why, Giovanno, why?'

And Giovanno says, 'As you no like my greeting, Hooky no like the way he was treated by the butcher.'

It is a parable about tolerance, I guess. Not that Target and Kmart seemed to be too into that. Those in charge took the book without reading it and then quickly took it off the shelves, probably still without reading it.

But I had my supporters, and in the most amazing of places – academia. Mark Read, the bloke who only just graduated from Form Two, is now the subject of much academic reviewing.

In the *Australian Journal of Studies*, Dr Deborah Hunn from Curtin University said this about *Hooky the Cripple* and me:

The transformation of ex-con Mark Brandon 'Chopper' Read – notorious, albeit apparently reformed, crook and hitman – into a successful writer may strike some cynics as yet another of those bizarre triumphs of celebrity over substance that have become all-too familiar in our surface-obsessed late-capitalist culture. Such a response, however, does not do justice to the skills of Read, whose forays into crime-writing require some serious consideration.

And this:

Powerfully framed by the gargoyles of Adam Cullen's bold, unsentimental illustrations, *Hooky the Cripple* is a short, punchy exercise in prose that spins the basic stuff of the Brothers Grimm et al. into a classic Australian theme: the defence of a little battler beset by bullies and wowsers.

And it gets even better:

There is a frankness here – and elsewhere – that suggests this is one tale that should not be selected for naptime reading to the kindergarten cohort. Nevertheless, Education Minister Brendan Nelson's reported outrage over talk of setting this text for secondary-school reading in Queensland seems hard to fathom. *Hooky* strikes me as unlikely to damage a generation raised on the unsentimental razor wit of *The Simpsons*, and it is certainly considerably less offensive than anything on show in *Big Brother Uncut*. Equally, unlike the latter opus horribilis, Read's text does actually have (whether you agree with it or not) a clearly defined ethical standpoint. Hooky's miserable lot exemplifies small-town hypocrisy in all its nastiness. Framed by the activities of the Inquisition, an ignorant bourgeois populace, flush with the dodgy ideological support of a distorted Christian piety, persistently torment Madonna's boy for his mother's past and his deformed looks (the latter thought to be evidence of God's punishment for the former).

The other adult fairytale is about a bloke who has sex with a polio victim that he found strung up on a barbed-wire fence. It is called *The Adventures of Rumsley Rumsflet* and was illustrated by Suzanne Soul.

Rumsley lifts the polio victim off the cattle fence after they have sex, and gets her dressed and takes her to her mother, who is formidable and has a shotgun in her hand.

He says, 'I know you must be very shocked but I love your daughter and have every intention of marrying her.'

201

The mother says, 'You are a gentleman, because the last cheeky bastard left her hanging on the fence.'

My father told me these stories when I was a kid, so I have them all in my head. I have another adult fairytale coming out soon.

So, all up, fourteen books, if you count this one. I guess that makes me a pretty successful author, even – thanks to Dr Deborah Hunn and a few others – a critically acclaimed one.

People always want to know what bits in my other books are true and which ones aren't. One of the people who asked me that question was Patrick Carlyon, from *The Bulletin*, a fine publication that is no longer being produced. I replied:

Once you pick up pen and paper, you can take people on a journey anywhere. The trouble is they come back later on and ask: 'Is that true?' I say: 'Who gives a shit?'

Or, as I put it on *Australian Story* when they asked me that same question: 'You can't ruin it for the viewers.'

There are a few things that I talk about for the first time in this book and that are true. And what Margaret has to say is the truth, as she has seen it over the years, too.

Which brings us to *Chopper* the movie, which was based on my books. Please turn the page.

CHAPTER 8

CHOPPER – A REVIEW

I've had plenty to say about the movie *Chopper*.

A blockbuster movie all over the world, it was, but I never got a cent.

But the person who really got burned the most by the movie was Margaret. Anyone watching it could have thought the main female character was based on Margaret, and the main female character is a heroin addict and a prostitute. She has never seen the funny side of the idea that, working for a phone company, she might have been a callgirl of sorts. And she has my sympathy.

Anyway, I've already said plenty of things about the movie to the media in the past, so I am going to hand over to Margaret Read for the ultimate critique of *Chopper*.

I can tell you now it will be better than anything David Stratton and Margaret Pomeranz could ever come up with.

MARGARET: I can't tell you how much I have been looking forward to finally getting to have my say about *Chopper*, the movie. When I hear all the favourable things that get said about it, I feel I must be the only person who dislikes it or disagrees with the way it was made. I couldn't even sit through it the first time without feeling totally humiliated and disgusted.

What was I watching, I wondered – a cross between *The Castle* and *Homicide*? Nothing was accurate. Yes, there were bits and pieces of my life and stories about the guy I knew and loved, and yet it was so far-fetched and sickening.

I couldn't see any humour, yet some of the patrons were laughing at the most delicate and saddest parts of Mark's life. His life was a difficult one from the start. He had a tough upbringing, including a father who deprived Mark of a normal life and took away his freedom from an early age. His father also had psychological problems and strange ideas about morals.

His mother was loving and normal, and did her very best to keep everything in perspective. But with a father like Mark's (whom Mark just adored and looked up to), no wonder Mark had no chance to get a grip on what was real, or what was right or best for him.

Unfortunately, it all got too much for Mark's mum and she decided to leave the Read household and make a life of her own. I am very close to Mark's mum and have been for many years. She is a lovely lady and lets me be who I am, and it comes naturally to me to open up to her.

We see things in the same light and are both very private people. She is a confidante who has helped me through my darkest days. As Mark has mentioned, she once gave me a gold pendant, a replica of the Victoria Cross, with the words 'For Valour' inscribed on it. I proudly wear it on my gold chain.

I know that Mark hasn't been too kind about his mum over the years, including in some places in this book. But I can only blame that on being brainwashed by his father. Mark and his mum remain in contact, and have lengthy and jovial conversations. I love hearing them both laugh; they are very witty and articulate. And he signs off by saying, 'Bye, Mum, I love you.'

Getting back to the movie, I really don't know where they drummed up the script from. I believe it was the director's idea of who Mark Read was, without making any attempt to work out why he was that person. The movie doesn't display any rhyme or reason for Mark's actions and violent days. To them, he was a gun-happy nuff nuff who liked to prey on other criminals. The hate seemed to come from Mark alone, giving the impression that all Mark wanted was a bloodbath.

They seemingly forgot that Mark wasn't always the instigator and that some of the guys he was in prison with used to plot against him. You have to consider why anyone would inflict so much pain on themselves. Mark had pain inflicted on him and he responded with more pain.

He must have told himself that it wasn't going to be like this forever and a day; that he wasn't going to be picked on while he had to serve twenty-three years. One thing I know is that he had to become as hard as the walls around him just to survive. Remarkably, his strategies worked better inside than they did outside. Maybe his institutionalisation gave him an extra edge there.

Certainly, living on the outside after his first release wasn't that easy for Mark. He had difficulties living in a world that was so full of rules he just couldn't fathom. Prison certainly had its own rules – both formal and informal. He was quite comfortable with both sets of rules.

But once he got out of prison, he really struggled. No matter what I said, or anyone advised him, he had been locked away for too many years to know how to conduct himself in a responsible way.

Therefore, he could only associate with the people he was most familiar with and resort to the way he had lived while he was in prison. That then meant he got up to no good and landed back in prison. In the case of his longest prison sentence – for kidnapping the judge – that meant he ended up back there just seven months after he was released. Mind you, he had been encouraged to go and commit the crimes he committed while he was out.

In the movie, the portrayal of crims who had been part of Mark's life was pretty accurate, but stories were intertwined, and two or three characters would be turned into one. Some characters were long dead before the time in the movie. Jimmy Loughnan never made it home, or even had a day pass, from Pentridge, having died in the Jika Jika fire in late 1987.

That really made me wonder how the audience even understood who was who and what was what, when Mark had never revealed who they were in his books. Basically, for anyone to know – well, you had to be part of that circle.

There was one thing that they totally gutted and that gutted me along with it. That, of course, was the portrayal of

Mark's girlfriend, Tanya. There was no such girl of that name. I had been his girlfriend from 1983. I visited Mark in Pentridge for years. When he got out of there for the last time, in 1991, we took off to live in Tasmania.

I can assure you I wasn't that girl Tanya. I was not a prostitute or a heroin addict. I had held respectable positions with two major phone companies, and always worked until Mark and I were married and I became a stay-at-home mum. The hurt is even deeper because I provided the only normality in Mark's life at that time.

In the movie, people with criminal convictions were allowed to keep their real identities. But I, a person with no criminal record, and no involvement in crime in any way, shape or form, had my reputation trashed.

And it got worse with the scene in which Mark bashed 'my' mother. Where on earth did they get that? My mother died in 1979. Sadly, very sadly, the two of them never met. I would have loved my mother to have met Mark.

I remember when I first found out about the way I had been portrayed in *Chopper*. I was at work when I received a phone call from a dear friend of mine, Billy Longley. The movie was in its first week of release, and he rang me to tell me I must go and see it, to see what they had done with my character. He told me he was absolutely disgusted. He said, 'Love, they have portrayed you in the lowest form possible.'

When I got home, where I could talk properly, I rang Billy back straightaway. He insisted I see the movie and take legal action.

Mark was in Risdon Prison in Tasmania and we were no longer together. He was seeing someone else and so was I.

And I was beginning to believe that he might have been behind my portrayal in the movie, to make things look better for him. I had no way of knowing then.

Billy, having recommended a lawyer to me, very kindly offered to underwrite my legal fees.

The lawyer looked at the movie closely and said to me, 'Margaret, anyone who knows you personally will know that it is totally untrue and know it is not you.'

'Yeah,' I said, 'but what about the rest of Australia?'

Incidentally, Eric Bana's tattoos from neck to stomach were all the same as Mark's, except that down the middle of his chest there was no mention of my name. They conveniently left that one out, because I would have had a very strong legal case against them if they had included the word 'Margaret' among Chopper's tattoos.

We did contact the producer and director for an explanation and they came up with some rubbish that Mark had other girlfriends while he was seeing me. Where do they get all this when they knew nothing about us?

Quite by coincidence, as I was writing this chapter, I came across the letters my solicitor wrote to the people involved in making *Chopper*. They make interesting reading.

Re: OUR CLIENT – MARGARET CASSAR
AN AUSTRALIA FILM FINANCE CORPORATION AND
MUSHROOM PICTURES FILM PRODUCED BY PARIAH
FILM – 'CHOPPER' – AUSTRALIAN RELEASE DATE
3RD AUGUST 2000

We advise that we act for the abovenamed Margaret Cassar (our client) who is an identifiable person in the above named film.

The person who is said to be 'Tanya' 'a working girl with a taste for amphetamines' and is described as a person who is suspected of being involved with a Western Suburbs drug-baron Neville Barton, and who is said to have had a longstanding relationship with 'Chopper' is clearly intended to depict our client's relationship with 'Chopper'.

Having regard to our client's longstanding relationship with 'Chopper' it is unlikely that any person who knows our client, 'Chopper' and their relationship would fail to identify our client as the character named as 'Tanya' and would ordinarily assume that our client was at the time of her relationship with 'Chopper'

   (a) a working girl
   (b) a person with a taste for amphetamines
   (c) a person suspected of having been involved
         with a Western Suburbs drug baron.

The longstanding relationship our client had with 'Chopper' necessarily points to our client being the person 'Tanya' since 'Chopper' had no long term relationship with other females.

Having regard to the description and identification of our client Margaret in the publication named 'Chopper 2 Hits and Memories' (Page 43) which names a lady that he has had a long time relationship with as 'Margaret', any person who knows our client and knows of our client's relationship with 'Chopper' is certain to identify the person named 'Tanya' in the film and will assume and regard our client as being

(a) a working girl

(b) had or has a taste for amphetamines

(c) was suspected of having been involved with a Western Suburbs drug baron Neville Barton (whoever that person may be).

Each of those assertions are untrue as our client was never:

(a) a working girl (meaning in the context of prostitute)

(b) a person with a taste for amphetamines in the context of a use of drugs

(c) a person of loose morals who is suspected to have had an association with a Western Suburbs drug baron.

Each of those are offensive, defamatory and a most slanderous assertion and description of our client who is a law abiding person who did not have and does not have any dealings or involvement in activities attributed to 'Tanya'.

In view of this our client requires that:

(a) the film in its present form not be circulated, publicly exhibited or displayed and that the film be removed from public exhibition and destroyed.

Or alternatively to mitigate our client's loss and damage our client seeks

(b) that any reference in the form of the character named 'Tanya' be deleted so that our client does not suffer the embarrassment, humiliation and public ridicule as being the person identified as 'Tanya'.

Of course none of those things happened. Outwardly, I moved on. Whenever I heard anyone talking about Mark or the movie, I remained silent.

There is another reason that I may have been portrayed in that way. When the movie was being made, Michele Bennett, the producer, called me at home. They must have known that Mark and I were no longer together. Being a private person – particularly back then – no one was going to get anything out of me as no one could get close to me. I had built up a wall when I returned to Melbourne from Tasmania and no one was going to get in, especially the movie crew.

I asked the question, 'What's in it for me?' I didn't really want anything; I just wanted to hear the answer.

The producer said there was no money because it was a low budget movie.

Oh yeah, I thought, *you're just doing it for the pleasure . . . right.* I said, 'Sorry, I won't be able or available to help you out.'

I remember saying to her that my ten-year relationship with Mark was over and it was a chapter of my life I would take with me to the grave. I would never have thought my relationship with Mark was going to end up on the big screen; it just doesn't happen that way after a break-up.

In my case it did.

I remember she also said, 'But you're a big part of his life.'

She got that right, but I wonder if my unwillingness to help caused them to punish me. If they did, they covered themselves well legally by saying the movie is an adaptation of Mark Read's life.

There were no complimentary passes to the movie for me, and no invitation to the premiere, just the load of rubbish

211

in it leaving me mentally and emotionally affected for some time. Mark wasn't invited to the premiere either, yet heaps of people went to it who were insignificant in, or even in no way connected to, Mark's life. That really hurt Mark, and hurts him to this day . . . not to have been invited to the premiere of a movie claiming to be about his life.

The only positive thing that has come out of all this is that Mark is able to make a living by telling his story on stage around Australia. He can also sell his creative artwork to people who have embraced the changes he has made and genuinely admire him for himself.

The only other explanation I can think of for the Tanya character is that the media and people generally just assume a typical underworld figure would have whores and strippers as girlfriends, that no other sort of woman would ever have them as partners. The truth is that most of the high-profile guys from that world have decent wives who are totally removed from it.

I really didn't deserve what *Chopper* did to me and neither does Roy.

As you can see, Margaret feels very strongly about the way she was misrepresented in the movie.

I have no real idea where that character Tanya came from. One of the people working on the movie said that he was a heroin addict for ten years, and he probably just imagined that everyone was on the needle. I have never taken heroin and I can assure you that Margaret never has either.

The only money I ever made from the movie was $27,000, and I gave that to the Royal Children's Hospital. Well, it actually went to the police's Bluey charity and they gave it to the Royal Children's Hospital. *Chopper* went on to make $67 million worldwide.

Another thing that really pisses me off is that Eric Bana, the bloke who played Chopper, really owes his whole international career to me. It was me who picked him out to play the part of Chopper Read.

Moviewise, he was just a plodder in *The Castle* until I nominated him to play me.

I met him at Glen Air when he was preparing for the part. We went out and got drunk together. He spent a couple of days with me, from memory. On the DVD's extras, there's this little bonus scene of Eric Bana and me together on the farm at Glen Air.

When the movie came out, it attracted a fair bit of high praise around the place. Michele Bennett, the producer, and Andrew Dominik, the director, rang to tell me they had received letters of congratulation from Quentin Tarantino; Madonna's then husband, Guy Ritchie; and James Ellroy, the crime fiction writer. Andrew Dominik kept those letters; I've never seen them, just had them read over the phone to me.

As Margaret also said, I didn't get invited to opening night. I remember the night *Chopper* cleaned up at the Australian Film Institute Awards. I didn't get invited to that bunfight either. I sat back in my trackie daks on the farm in Tassie with a bourbon and Coke and watched it on television. When Eric got his award, he said he wouldn't cry because Mark Read wouldn't like that. Well Eric, as you can see there's quite a bit I don't like about *Chopper* and the way it was made, but you having a cry in front of your mates is about the least of it.

CHAPTER 9

PAINTER AND PUBLIC SPEAKER – MAKING AN HONEST LIVING

When I appeared in the magistrates court in 2007, charged with a minor driving offence, my wonderful solicitor, Bernie Balmer, described my occupation as that of a painter and public speaker. Now, all of Bernie's words on my behalf are silky and eloquent but these have a special place for me – 'My client is these days, Your Worship, a painter and public speaker.'

Gone in one fell swoop was 'ex-crim', 'standover man' and all the other things that you usually hear Chopper Read described as. And 'painter and public speaker' certainly has a nicer ring to it than 'painter and docker' doesn't it?

When I came back to Melbourne, I had to find a legitimate way of making a living. That was one of the conditions Margaret had put on us getting back together: I couldn't return to my old ways of getting money.

Over the years, I've had a lot of what were probably really good business ideas, but I've never been that good with the money side of things. Margaret reckons that I don't know the difference between $50 and $500, all I know is that it is money and there to be spent. I suppose my record at various casinos proves that.

When it comes to business deals, too often I have found myself getting into schemes and partnerships where I get the rough end of the pineapple. That was probably the case when I joined the public-speaking circuit, or circus – it's a bit of both.

I had become pretty good at public speaking from having joined the debating club while in Risdon Prison. I ended up as secretary of the club, which was called the Spartan Debating Club. I only joined when they first invited me to because you got to stay out of your cell till eight pm, and have a cup of tea and a biscuit after the debate was over.

The first time I went along, I just listened in. I thought, 'Well, this is all right,' and so I joined up. I think, all up, they found my arguments, no matter the subject, to be very good.

We would debate with Toastmasters and various other debating groups from around Hobart, including the University Debating Club, who would all come out to Risdon Prison. In the early days of the club, I am told, the debates were a bit rudimentary. But, as the numbers of lawyers and accountants put away for diddling their books and clients grew, so too did the quality of the debates. Visitors from the various clubs would be greeted at the door with great cordiality by a Launceston accountant who got caught cooking the books of that city's landed gentry.

There were some pretty interesting types in the University Debating Club: clever people like Tim Lester, who was with the ABC in Tasmania but is now a parliamentary reporter in Canberra. The Eastern Shore Baptist Debating Society was another group that used to come and visit.

I remember that one of the topics for debate was whether Australia should become a republic. I was on the pro-republic side, though I really couldn't have given a rat's arse, then or now, about whether Australia becomes a republic. As I've said before, I think the idea of becoming a republic is a Labor Party plot to cover for the fact that all the fridges are empty. But once I found out which side of the debate I was on, I got fervently behind republicanism.

When young Patrick Carlyon interviewed me for *The Bulletin* back in 2002, I think I pretty well summed it all up:

Once I've got a camera in front of me I should be locked up in a cupboard. I lie my head off. I could be the minister for propaganda for the Nazi Party or the Communist Party with equal fervour. The reason I'm on telly and sound like I have so much conviction is because I have no convictions about anything at all. I believe I could have done well in politics.

Another topic we debated was whether David Boon should become the next governor of Tasmania. I had a number of arguments against it. At that stage, I was being held at the Governor's Pleasure. Having Boonie, a man who had tried all his sporting life to stay 'in', decide whether I should be let 'out' just didn't seem right. I was able to state as part of the debate that Boonie was a reader of my books, something he did between beers while flying around the nation from one Test venue to another.

There was probably only one topic that I really felt strongly about: should Australia abolish all gun laws? I was on the side that said we should and, I tell you, I bloody well believed in that one. And we won!

So I had developed a bit of prowess as a public speaker before Headley Gritter, from Melbourne radio station 3RRR, introduced me to Mark 'Jacko' Jackson. By the way, Headley was a producer of the movie *Trojan Warrior*. I had a cameo, as a bloke by the name of Erik Bana. Ha ha! I went to Triple R to meet up with Headley and the star of the movie, Stan 'The Man' Longinidis, and to watch a preview.

Headley and the director, Salik Silverstein, had created the role of Trojan Warrior especially for Stan 'The Man' Longinidis, the eight-time heavyweight kick-boxing champion of the world. Stan started out working in IT in Melbourne but resigned to concentrate on his kickboxing career. He went to America and fought against some of the biggest names in the sport, including Branko Cikatić, Arthur 'Mr C' Charlie, Grant Barker and Dennis Alexio. In 1992, he beat Alexio in front of a packed stadium of 10,000 people in Melbourne, by breaking his leg after just six seconds. A bit disappointing for the crowd. Probably a bit disappointing for Alexio, too. After he gave up kickboxing, Stan 'The Man' Longinidis went into acting.

Mark 'Jacko' Jackson was a former AFL footballer and, if you ask him, a boxer too. In *Trojan Warrior*, he played the role of Zork. After Stan and Headley introduced me to Jacko, he told me I should get involved with him in public speaking.

He booked a tour of South Australia for the pair of us and then said I should also come to Perth with him, for another twenty-four shows. I told him I would do Adelaide but wasn't promising anything after that. In fact, I had pretty much said no to the trip to Perth. On the way to Adelaide, though, I decided to do it.

When I told Jacko so on the plane, he shouted out, 'Yeah,' and punched the air like he'd just kicked another goal for Geelong. He had already booked the shows in Perth.

I later found out he was desperate for money. People had got sick and tired of listening to him talk. It had got to the stage where he couldn't get two people to turn up to his shows. But he knew he could make a fortune out of getting around with me. I could fill up a room, something that I did for five and a half years, and can still do.

At Margaret's and my wedding, Mark 'Jacko' Jackson made a speech in our honour. He said that before the first gig in Adelaide, he had been very worried about how I would go. That was because the first time that Mark 'Jacko' Jackson had teamed up with Warwick

Capper on the speaking circuit, Capper had managed just three minutes, way short of the allotted forty-five. That left Jacko with a lot of time to fill.

He said that for our first night, he had Peter Bosustow, another former AFL player, who was the MC, ready with a stack of questions to help me through. 'Mark got up and he spoke for forty-eight minutes on his first night, which is unbelievable,' Mark 'Jacko' Jackson said. 'He is virtually the best after-dinner speaker in Australia as we speak.' And is eight years later, as you're reading this!

The partnership with Mark 'Jacko' Jackson ended when we had a bust-up over money. I was on a set wage and thought he was too, but then I discovered he regularly got more than me.

You can imagine how I felt when I found out what was going on. So I sacked him.

I did it at our second-last show, at the Comics Lounge in Melbourne, telling the audience that I would not be working with Mark 'Jacko' Jackson anymore. We had one more show to do, at the Palais in St Kilda; we did it, and that was it. Mark 'Jacko' Jackson thought he could talk me into coming back, but he couldn't. It must have been very embarrassing for him to be sacked on stage.

I then went on the speaking circuit with Roger Rogerson. Even though he is a former New South Wales police detective and I have lived most of my life in Victoria and Tasmania, we have a few things in common. For example, he investigated the Toecutter Gang murder in Sydney. I'd done a bit of toecutting myself.

Roger ended up going to prison after being convicted for perverting the course of justice and giving false evidence to the New South Wales Police Integrity Commission in 1999. Up until then, he'd been one of the most decorated policemen in the state. He'd won the Peter Mitchell Trophy. This is not named after the Melbourne newsreader who came to Margaret's and my wedding; it's the biggest annual award for a police officer in New South Wales. Roger Rogerson got that in 1980, for his arrest of armed robber Gary Purdey.

Roger Rogerson also shot and killed drug dealer Warren Lanfranchi. A coroner found he had been acting in the line of duty. But Lanfranchi's girlfriend, Sallie-Anne Huckstepp, a heroin addict and prostitute, claimed that Roger had murdered him. Another mutual acquaintance of ours, Neddy Smith, backed up her story. Sallie-Anne Huckstepp ended up dead in Sydney's Centennial Park.

Roger Rogerson was also charged with the attempted murder of another policeman, Michael Drury, but was acquitted. He was also charged but then acquitted of heroin dealing with another mutual acquaintance, Dennis Allen.

We worked together as the Wild Colonial Psychos.

So, with me having a movie about me, all these best-selling books and now a place on the public-speaking circuit, I had become a bit of a celebrity. Now, that can be a bit of a nuisance at times, but it also has its upside.

One of the big nuisances is that people think they can charge you more for things. When Margaret's hairdresser found out she was married to Chopper Read, they must have thought, 'Well, he had that movie made about him, so he's got plenty of money.' So, the next time Margaret went there, they charged her $200. She never went back.

One of the upsides of being a bit famous is that you get to meet other famous people. Joe Bugner – Aussie Joe Bugner, the former heavyweight boxer – has always been a hero of mine. When I met him, he turned out to be a wonderful bloke. I have always admired him for the fact that he had never been set on his arse in his whole career, not even by Muhammad Ali. He boxed Joe Frazier and Muhammad Ali. He lost twice to Ali but both times on points. So, he went twenty-seven rounds with one of the greatest boxers ever and never got sat on his arse. I never saw Aussie Joe Bugner fight in the flesh, but I bet a lot of money on him over the years.

Then there was the time I ended up on stage with the Red Hot Chili Peppers. One night, Margaret and I were leaving the Quay West Hotel in Brisbane when all these blokes started coming into the foyer. Margaret said that they looked like roadies, and went and asked them who they were with. Then one of them saw me standing in the foyer and asked Margaret if I was Chopper Read. When she said yes, they all wanted to come and have their picture taken with me and get an autograph. On the flight from America to Australia for their tour, they had all watched *Chopper*.

Anyway, they took our number and said they'd catch up with us when they got to Melbourne. I told Margaret that it was bullshit – that they weren't really roadies for the Red Hot Chili Peppers and were just pulling her leg. But, sure enough, when they got to Melbourne, they phoned and asked us to come to the concert.

And there we were, Margaret and me, sitting up on the stage, right next to Flea's grandmother, Muriel Boxthorpe, who was in a wheelchair. Michael 'Flea' Balzary is the bass player with the Red Hot Chili Peppers and lived for a while with his grandmother in Mount Waverley when he was growing up.

And on the other side of us was Jane Barnes, Jimmy's wife. We spent a lot of time with Jimmy that weekend. We were at his concert on the Friday night, and then we were at the Red Hot Chili Peppers. On the Monday, I went along to one of Jimmy's book signings. He has also invited me to his home in Botany in Sydney for a meal. The Barneses are just a really nice family and it is a privilege to have been able to meet them.

Another band I have got to meet is the Alabama 3, who perform the theme song to *The Sopranos*. They're not from Alabama and there aren't three of them. There's a whole stack of them, and they're from England, Scotland and Wales. Their harmonica player is a bloke by the name of Nick Reynolds. He made a bust of me; as well as being a great harmonica player, he's a pretty good sculptor. Nick did a book featuring some of his busts, called *Heroes and Villains*, which included a bust of Ronnie Biggs, one of the Great Train Robbers. His bust of me was a pretty special gift, particularly when you know about Nick Reynolds's family history. He is the son of the mastermind of the Great Train Robbery, Bruce Richard Reynolds. The Alabama 3 wrote a song called 'Have You Seen Bruce Richard Reynolds?', and Nick's old man actually performed on it.

It's a great story, the Great Train Robbery. For all the young people out there, it happened in England on 8 August 1963. Bruce Richard Reynolds and his gang got away with 2.6 million quid, a bloody lot of money in those days. It's a bloody lot of money these days. Interestingly, though, pound for pound, it wasn't as big a haul as when Frank Gardiner and his boys held up the Eugowra stage coach – Eugowra being a town in the west of New South Wales.

They only got 3000 quid in cash, but topped that up nicely with seventy-seven kilograms of gold. It was the time of the New South Wales gold rush. Some of the bullion was retrieved because it was too heavy for the getaway horses to carry, but a lot wasn't. Eventually, they caught Frank Gardiner and he did time for the robbery, but he never told anyone where he put his gold. When he got out of prison, he went to America, where he died.

One day, these two American blokes turned up in the central west of New South Wales, and purchased a couple of spades and a crowbar and disappeared into the bush. The blokes were never seen again, but a bloody big hole was found, with a couple of spades and a crowbar next to it.

The story goes that it was Frank Gardiner's sons. Apparently, what Frank Gardiner did back then is still some sort of a record for an armed hold-up, and since nobody has ever really admitted how much money was involved in the Great Bookie Robbery in Melbourne – well, who can argue.

The Great Train Robbery was a pretty big one, too, or a pretty Biggs one. Ronnie Biggs probably got a lot more publicity than Bruce Richard Reynolds, but Reynolds was the real mastermind. The train was what the poms called a TPO, or travelling post office. It had twelve carriages and nearly eighty people on it, and went from Glasgow to London. The mail was put on the train in Scotland and they collected more mail on the way to London. There were bags hanging on the side of the tracks and, as the train flew past, it hooked them in. One carriage was for the registered mail, and that's where all the money was. Because the day of the Great Train Robbery followed a bank holiday, there was more money in the carriage than normal.

Reynolds's plan was a pretty good one. The gang stopped the train by covering up the green lights and using their own red one, which was attached to a battery. There were fifteen blokes in the gang. Between them, they got 124 sacks off the train and drove to a farm they had just bought, to count the loot.

As part of Reynolds's plan, they had cut all the phone lines around where they did the robbery. It was an hour and a half after the robbery before the coppers found out about it, when someone from the train walked all the way into the next town. They were pretty smart coppers, too, it seems. One of the robbers had told the people on the train not to move for at least half an hour. So, the coppers reckoned that wherever the robbers were, it was within half an hour of the scene of the crime.

The farm was deserted by the time the police got to it as part of their search, but they found plenty of evidence of recent activities. There was a truck and other vehicles, mail bags and a Monopoly board. Apparently, the gang played Monopoly after doing the robbery, but did so with real money.

Most of them ended up being caught, and Bruce Richard Reynolds did ten years. He became a bit of a celebrity criminal after that and wrote a book called *Autobiography of a Thief*. A few of the others became celebrity thieves too. The whole world knows about Ronnie Biggs, who ended up in Adelaide and Melbourne for a bit after he escaped just fifteen months into his thirty-year sentence.

Phil Collins starred in a move called *Buster* that was based on the life of Ronald 'Buster' Edwards, another member of the Reynolds gang. He went to Mexico but eventually turned himself in. He ended up selling flowers outside a train station in London, and finally killed himself.

I believe there have been three movies made about the Great Train Robbery and there's been the song by the Alabama 3. Is that living off the proceeds of crime? I don't think so, and thanks for the bust, Nick.

Being Chopper Read has allowed me to meet other famous people too: the lead singer from Jamiroquai; Danny Green, the boxer; and one of the Bra Boys, Koby Abberton. He's just beginning his professional surfing career again, after getting off some charge in New South Wales.

Besides *Chopper* and my appearance in *Trojan Warrior*, I put out a DVD of my own last year. It was called *Fatbelly*. I said to this bloke, 'Get a video camera and we will go out in your garage, and I will just be talking to a couple of mates and answering questions.' I said we'd sell the finished product on the Internet.

He got fifty percent of the first sales but is only getting fifteen percent now. I've cut him back. He's probably got me back a bit, though, by putting up on YouTube a video of me falling asleep during the filming. I can fall asleep anywhere these days.

I've also done community service work. In 2001 I made an advertisement for the Pedestrian Council of Australia. I donated my time, as did the advertising agency Saatchi and Saatchi. They sent some bloke from Saatchi out to our house in Collingwood, along with what he thought was a hard-hitting script, and I said, 'I will give you a bloody hard-hitting script.'

And I did. I took off my shirt so I could show all my scars to the camera. Then I said:

When I was in prison, I got, er, slashed down the face, my ears cut off.

I had a claw hammer put through my brain just here.

Cut-throat razors here, here.

Eight-and-a-half-inch butcher's knife there.

Icepick there.

Icepick up the back there.

If you drink and you drive . . . and you're unfortunate enough to hit somebody, you want to pray to God you don't ever go to prison.

I did another version in which I said not to drink and drive, 'otherwise you'll end up a murderer maggot like me'.

The ad was so hard-hitting, it got banned in some places. And it won a Golden Lion award. If I'd stuck to the script from Saatchi and Saatchi, it wouldn't have gone anywhere.

I also did an ad that was against violence to women. That's another reason I am pissed off about *Chopper*, the movie – that they had me hitting women. Chopper Read never hits women!

I got into painting after Adam Cullen, the artist, did a portrait of me. Adam's a pretty smart sort of bloke and he's become a good friend of mine. He's studying for a PhD and is a lecturer in art history at the University of New South Wales.

Anyway, his painting of me was a runner-up in the Archibald Prize in 2002. I've been painted for the Archibald Prize five times. I can't work out why I am so popular.

I remember that one of the first times I went to visit Adam Cullen, I looked up and there was this particular painting on the wall. I must have thought it was all right, I suppose, and then Adam told me he had just sold two similar ones to Elton John, for $25,000. I thought, 'How long has this shit been going on?' So I went out and bought two canvases, two paintbrushes and some acrylic paints, and I've never looked back.

I remember once saying that I was a graphic artist, because my paintings are pretty fuckin' graphic.

Ha ha!

Not everyone was happy, though, that Chopper Read was trying to make an honest living as a painter.

All the do-gooders came out of the woodwork when the State Library of Victoria bought a self-portrait of mine called *Tasteful Old Criminal* for $1450. They bought it as part of something they were doing about Ned Kelly because the painting had a bit of Ned in it, along with the words 'Regret Nothing' and 'Ned 21'.

But the State Library went into bat for itself pretty strongly, led by a bloke by the name of Shane Carmody. 'The painting is important to the collection because it represents a contemporary interpretation of Ned Kelly and the State Library has a very important collection of Ned Kelly material,' he said to the media. 'We feel it is important to add to that collection so that people can see how Ned Kelly is interpreted through the years.'

But another bloke, Noel McNamara, from the Crime Victims Support Association, said it was 'disgraceful' that government money was going to a convicted criminal. 'I am quite surprised that the government could let money go to . . . I suppose you'd call it a fund for old criminals,' Mr McNamara said. Then he added, 'The nearest Chopper comes to Van Gogh is he cut his ears off.'

Ha bloody ha.

The Premier of Victoria, Steve Bracks, came out on my side too.

So, in the end, all the publicity probably helped drive up the price of my paintings. Having said that, I haven't sold any to bloody Elton John for $25,000 yet. The best price I have got for one of my paintings is $8500. But that's not the highest price that has ever been paid for one of my paintings.

In May 2010 I travelled to the Western Australian town of Newman, to do a speaking engagement. Newman is located about 1200 kilometres north of Perth. It is nine kilometres north of the Tropic of Capricorn and in the Pilbara region. About 4000 people live there and it is a nice town that stands out from the red desert all around it.

There's a bloody big crater near the town, which they reckon was caused by a meteorite. Either that, or Frankie Waghorn's been there and punched a bloody big hole in the ground. It's a mining town and I suppose mining's going all right at the moment, particularly in Western Australia.

It is a real thrill to get invitations to go to places like Newman, places that ten years ago I don't think I would ever have thought of visiting. It's a long way to Newman, but I've come a long way to being a new man myself, I suppose.

Before I left for Newman, I did a painting that I donated to the people who were organising this speaking engagement, to raise money for the Royal Flying Doctors Service. It sold at auction for $14,000. I was very pleased to have done my bit to help the Royal Flying Doctors Service. Obviously, one of the miners in the audience had a much different view of my painting from some of Melbourne's, allegedly finest, art critics. A bloke in *The Age* wrote a story called 'Who Is Going to Tell Chopper Read His Paintings Are Awful?' I'll bet that journo has never sold a painting for eighty-five cents, let alone $8500, or $14,000.

I've had a few goes at Ned Kelly during my career as an artist. In one painting, I gave him breasts. That caused a bit of a stir.

I always thought Ned Kelly was half a fag.

He was too close to that Aaron Sherritt for my liking. There was definitely something a bit funny about old Ned and Aaron. Sherritt ended up dying pretty young. He was killed by another member of the Kelly gang, Joe Byrne, after he dobbed them in to the police. Sherritt was letting the police live in his house while they were spying on the Kelly gang.

I don't reckon it was Ned Kelly who wrote the Jerilderie Letter, I reckon it was Aaron Sherritt. Ned Kelly was illiterate. I know he was supposed to have dictated it to Joe Byrne, but I reckon all the correct grammar and big words sound more like Aaron Sherritt.

You might not believe it but I'm not all that happy with people comparing me to Ned Kelly. At my wedding, even my good friend Adam Cullen called me a modern-day Ned Kelly, but I don't like being called any kind of Ned Kelly. I am not a great Australian folk hero. I don't bother thinking too much about what I am.

Yeah, I've become a bit famous and that's been pretty handy in helping me derive an honest income. Love it or hate it, *Chopper* did that for me. My books are good, but it was really the movie that made me famous around the world.

As I've said, a few blokes have ripped me off along the way but I reckon that in my new manager, Andrew Parisi, I've found a bloke I can really trust. Margaret trusts him too. She reckons he can see my sensitive side as well as my dark one.

Thinking back, as you do when you write your autobiography, I've been involved in a few other business ventures. Chopper's Nuts – now, that was an interesting name. A lot of people back in H Division thought Chopper was nuts, mad enough to need a good stabbing . . . That reminds me, one of the nurses who looked after me after one of those incidents in Pentridge is now living in Hamilton, Victoria, and she came to see me after one of my shows there. That was a nice gesture.

I've done a couple of CDs too. The first one was called *Interview with a Madman*. It was a rap song. I'm not really into rap music, but this one was all right. It was done with a bloke called Jaydub. He was okay. I say that because I am also not a big fan of some of these American rappers who try to act like they're gangsters. A lot of them are pretenders.

Then there was *Chopper the Musical*. I am trying to sing a bit on that but have left most of it to a bloke who calls himself Big Haz. He is a Melbourne MC and producer. He's the first hip hop artist from Australia to work with the American legends of hip hop and earn their respect. Well, that's what he tells me – and I believe him. He's well known for the storytelling in his music, his lyricism and his production. His debut solo album, *Larger Than Life*, was released in July 2010.

'Every Day Above Ground Is a Good One' is one of the songs from *Chopper the Musical*. It really tested Big Haz's ability to write lyrics. I rang him up the day before we had to record the song and said, 'I hope you've got something to rhyme with "Gangitano".'

Big Haz came through beautifully.

Here are all the lyrics, starting with verse one, with me on vocals:

What I like to do is get a blowtorch, tickle a bloke's feet, get the smell of burnt flesh in the air.
When Chopper Read's got you in a lounge room with your hands nailed to a coffee table and he says where's the fuckin' money?
Don't scream injustice, you weak prick! Just gimme the fuckin money, or you'll end up on the fucking missing list!
Hahaha.
Big Haz and Chopper straight out of maximum security H Division. A butcher's knife isn't made for slicing up lamb cutlets, I'll put one through your fuckin head!
Then you will be fuckin dead! Hahahaha.

Big Haz then takes over the vocals for a bit:

Thugged out like Pentridge Prison,
When Chopper was choppin' up convicts with vein incisions in H Division,
A Stanley knife is a manly vice, that will madly slice, and badly blind, behind bars we improvise.
You sleep at night, I'm in ur mind, with demon eyes,
Shanking your spleen inside with a concrete knife three feet wide,
Duck when the fo' bangs,
Gangsta like Chopper in South Yarra in the 70s with the Surrey Road Gang,

Twenty-one gun salute by Chopper and Dave the Jew,
Amazing proof, that Cowboy was a thug that's razor proof.
Twenty-two blades in you,
When you're too lazy to look behind you in the shower,
And two inmates are raping you,
With homemade tools.
In a blood and guts gang war I'm physically fearless,
Gun in hand situation I'm a criminal genius,
With the .410 shotty sparkin',
$^4/10$ths of your body the sharks did,
The $^6/10$ths up in Darwin.

Then me on the vocals again:

Me, Mad Charlie, and my little Greek mate Frank ruled
St Kilda like Al ruled Carlton . . . But we're not dead,
hahahahahaha.
We were armed to the teeth, if Mad Charlie gave the
go-ahead they'd all be dead. You should have seen the
hand grenades we fuckin' had, hahahaha.

Back to Big Haz:

The most rugged cunt,
Confessions from the Australian underworld's most
feared headhunter,
Don't Front!
A toecutter, gang kidnapped a payroll bandit,
And put him under heavy questioning for seventy-five
grand
Removed all the toes on his left foot, he laughed loud,
Skinned the tattoo off his back and he passed out

Couldn't revive him, he must have had a honey,
No one would go through the tortures of Hell to protect
money
We went to her crib and made an offer,
We pretended he was alive . . . 'Why?' . . . to get the
money off her
If foes tangle, domes mangled, at four angles,
The .410 bangs you, at Chevron or Bojangles
Bag me and I'mma stab yours, with a fat sword, and
bash yours,
With a raging left hook like Frankie Waghorn
Big Haz and Chopper, how is justice measured?
At Risdon held at the Governor's Pleasure? . . . Come on

Me again:

If you wear designer suits with that Mafia bravado,
You'll end up dead like Gangitano hahaha
Nick Apostolidis, sure I burnt his house down,
Why not? I love a sunburnt bloody country hahaha . . .
Fuck him!

Back to Big Haz:

A blowtorch is the preferred method of success,
To you it's a foul stench, to me it smells fresh
Burnt flesh makes you change your mind, kid,
You didn't know where the money was, now you told
me where to find it
Drug dealing is a dangerous game,
When Australia's finest toecutter knows where you live,
And where your money lays

Underworld executioner, blood splattered career,
Street fighter, standover man, I BRING FEAR!
Collingwood streets, Chopper Read territory,
VBs and mini Macks, meat cleaver, your back
Reach for a piece when Francini fires,
Bullets hit your dome quicker than screeching Lambor-
ghini tyres
Even if you wanted, you couldn't stop it,
Wait in your garage and you'll get dropped, when the
gun's poppin'
That's no disrespect, it's just a fact,
If people want you dead, they'll get you when you're
most relaxed
The Overcoat Gang at Melbourne's Blue Stone College,
Icepicks and wad cutters through your dome, pay
homage,
Big Haz and Chopper, Melbourne's finest,
No ears, just some blokes with a lot of priors Ha!

And, one last time with feeling, it's me again:

In the Overcoat Gang we wore overcoats in the middle of
summer. It was FUCKIN HOT!
We were hiding iron bars and hammers up our sleeves. If
you don't believe me ask Dennis fuckin Allen hahaha did
we give it to that bastard!
That's right, Big Haz and Chopper hahaha
Ay, Big Haz, I got the .410 and the cigars, let's have a
smoke.
This is Mark Brandon Chopper Read, I'm a working class
genius.

This is my life I'm getting the fuck out of here!

Come on, Frankie, grab the gun, let's go, let's go, fuckin get 'em Hahaha

Don't forget the fuckin axe! Don't forget the fuckin meat cleaver! Hahahaha

Don't forget the fuckin ammo either. Remember last time when you forgot the fuckin ammo? That was very embarrassing, Frank! We had to hit 'em all nite on the head with a fuckin hammer!

Never forget the fuckin ammo, Frank! Oh never forget the fuckin ammo! Hahahaha

Frank Deaney –

This is Frank, I watch Chopper's back, so stay away or I'll break your fuckin back!

Simon and Garfunkel, eat your hearts out; Big Haz and me are the best duo ever. I don't think the CD sold all that well, though; perhaps we should have done our own version of 'Bridge Over Troubled Water'. You can still buy *Chopper the Musical* via the Internet. What are you fucken waiting for? Give me the fucken money!

With all these products out and about, I have decided to trademark the name Chopper Read. I wonder if I can use that to be able to walk into Michael Gudinski's office and say, 'Get all those fucken *Chopper* DVDs off the shelves!'

I might put the wind up the *Ronnie Johns Show* people too. This young comedian, Heath Franklin, has, I'm sure, been making a pretty good living out of impersonating me all over the place. The funny thing is, when I was doing my roadshows with Jacko and co, Franklin would always seem to have been there just before us. The *Ronnie Johns Show* would be charging eighty-five dollars to get in and we were only charging thirty-five. So, it was cheaper to see the real Chopper Read than to see the fake one with the high-pitched voice, who still had ears. Oh well, imitation is the sincerest form of flattery, but I would have preferred money.

Another moneymaking idea – back in 2003, I think this was – was Chopper Read wines. A bloke by the name of Andrew Roper came up to Jacko and me and asked us what we thought of the idea. Well, we must have thought it was all right because, all of a sudden, there was all this wine.

But Jacko quit the day after the company started. He wasn't prepared to carry a carton of wine across the street, so there was no chance of him carrying cartons of wine into bottle shops. I was pretty happy that Jacko quit, though, because he was always a bit of a nuisance.

Anyway, Andrew Roper conned this winemaker into producing six hundred dozen bottles of wine. He sold plenty of them too, but Jacko and I didn't see a penny.

Andrew Roper also had the idea of a Chopper Read beer. That was a bloody good idea and the beer sold pretty well. It had 5.6 percent alcohol, making it the strongest lager manufactured in Australia.

The beer sales made $60,000 gross but we didn't get our share.

That left me being owed $30,000 on top of the $10,000 I was already out of pocket for start-up costs when we went into business together.

A year later, Andrew came to me and said he had new people who were ready to put money into the venture, and gave me $14,000 and bought the company back from me. And he gave me a bottle of Grange Hermitage.

Anyway, what I've done hasn't always been a roaring success, but Mark Read has been able to make an honest living the past eight years or so. And I'm still in big demand as an after-dinner speaker.

Painter, public speaker, peanut promoter, wine merchant, rapper, writer: probably not as exciting as what I was up to in the old days, but it all keeps Margaret pretty happy.

CHAPTER 10

THE FREEMASONS AND MY TATTOOS

I got my first tattoo when I was seventeen.

I don't know why I did it. Back then, a lot of times, one thing just led to another.

I can't even remember now which one of my tattoos I got first. I do know, however, which is the most famous: the one on my bum that says, 'I LOVE ITA BUTTROSE'. Ita Buttrose is a pretty famous woman in Australia, but how her name came to be tattooed on Chopper Read's bum is an interesting story.

For a long time, she was editor of the *Australian Women's Weekly*. That was one of the few magazines we were allowed to read in prison; that, *Reader's Digest* and the *National Geographic*. So, Jimmy Loughnan and I set up the Pentridge branch of the Ita Buttrose Fan Club. And where else would you put a tattoo of Ita Buttrose but on your butt?

I wonder how her kids, Kate and Ben, are getting on these days. She used to write about them all the time in the *Women's Weekly*. And we used to read about them all the time and discuss the goings-on in the Buttrose family. I did hear Kate and Ben have both recently had children of their own and so Ita is a grandmother. I also heard recently that her nephew has gone to prison for selling cocaine. Drugs ruining everything again.

I know Ita didn't mind having a Pentridge fan club. I once saw her interviewed on television and saying she was okay with it.

One time, while I was having a drink in a Melbourne pub, a bloke had a crack at me for having a tattoo about Ita Buttrose on my bum. In fact, he said something pretty insulting about Ita, who, to us, was something of a saint, keeping us all informed in the *Women's Weekly* about her happy family life.

I said to this bloke, 'You can't say that sort of stuff about Ita.'

He told me to get stuffed.

So, I put my finger into his eye and took out his eyeball. I put it into my beer and I drank it down in one go. His eyeball tasted bloody awful.

Since getting my first tattoo at seventeen, I have pretty much ended up with tattoos all over my body, something that a lot of people would know. After all, I've been photographed often enough with my shirt off, on the covers of books and DVDs and so on. There's even a shoe shop in Melbourne that copied a photo of me in its advertising. They replaced me with a young woman and they put shoes instead of guns in her hands. Very clever, I thought.

All up, I have around 200 tattoos, including the ones I tried to burn off with a blowtorch. They tell me there are new and improved ways of getting rid of tattoos these days. Can't say I am all that interested, either way.

What nobody has known is that four of my tattoos are highly secret symbols of the Freemasons. On the inside of my left forearm are the words 'SUBLIME SONS OF HIRAM ABRIFF'. On the other side are the words 'KNIGHTS OF THE BRAZEN SERPENT'. At the top of my forearm is a triangle with '12' written on it and '1717' written underneath it. The symbol represents the Triangle of 12. My grandfather sat on the Triangle of 12. This is the worldwide ruling body for the Masonic Lodges. It is made up of twelve members of the Masonic Lodges who are Thirty-third Degree Masons, the highest rank that can be achieved. Most Masons aren't even aware that there is a Grand Lodge higher than that of Master Mason or Third Degree.

My father was a member of the Grand Lodge. He rose to the rank of Knight of the Brazen Serpent, or the Fifteenth Degree. When he achieved the rank of Third Degree Master Mason, my father got me into the Lodge, as a Lewis. I was fifteen years of age. I was seconded by two of Dad's friends who were both Third Degree Masons.

As a Lewis, I was taught certain code words, handshakes, written symbols and so on. There were certain ways to address and greet a stranger; how to say hello, how to say goodbye.

I couldn't enter the Lodge as a full member until I was twenty-one and, as I was told, should I find myself falling foul of the law between becoming a Lewis and reaching twenty-one, I would not be able to enter the Lodge at all.

However, once you're in the Lodge, you're in it forever. Having been taught all the signs, greetings and verbal expressions, you cannot be expelled. You just cannot enter a lodge again.

A lot of people probably don't know that disgraced former New South Wales policeman Roger Rogerson is a First Degree Mason. He entered the Blue Lodge as an apprentice. Because he's fallen foul of the law, he enters a different chapter of the Masonic Lodge, one that is unseen and unheard. It is called the 'Brethren – Black – Chapter Ancient Charge V1.4'.

I have tattooed on my right forearm 'Ancient Charge V1.4'. This is the oath of secrecy that all Masons swear. It is a solemn oath of silence or death. No true Mason will ever break this ancient charge. So, why did I have these tattoos put on my body? Well, it was my way of freaking out Dad, and it did. He said one day I could find myself dead with my arms cut off if I was not careful, if the wrong people ever found out.

I said to him, 'How will they ever find out, Dad?'

Ha ha.

I suppose writing about it for the first time in a book might be one way.

Ha ha!

CHAPTER 11

UNDERBELLY IS A LOT OF...

Underbelly, the television franchise, is a load of shit, really. At best, you've got eighty percent fiction, twenty percent fact.

For a start, I doubt that any criminal has ever really had such a wild and extravagant sex life as any of the *Underbelly* characters are depicted as having. There are more tits than you would see in an aviary. And I don't believe any of the women the characters were supposed to be having sex with were a quarter as good looking as the actresses in *Underbelly*.

So, that's my review of *Underbelly*. It's all bullshit, except the twenty percent that's not. And they got that much right because they bothered to seek the advice of one Mark Brandon Read.

Having said all that, I tip my lid to the president of my favourite football club for knowing a good story when he saw it. Eddie McGuire was in charge of Channel Nine up in Sydney, and the pinstriped Sydney types didn't think much of him, his crime being that he came from Melbourne – and probably earned more than them too.

But Eddie argued very strongly that the stories about the gangland killings that had been going on in Melbourne would make a good television series. And if anyone ever overheard Eddie getting stuck into the production team after something went wrong on *The Footy Show*, they would know he can be a fearsome opponent in an argument.

They apparently have a saying for this sort of thing up in Sydney – BIM, Big In Melbourne.

Well, the ratings for the first series of *Underbelly* proved what bad judges they were. It was Big In Australia.

The show's success was helped by its not being able for legal reasons to go to air in Melbourne. It is a fascinating aspect of human nature that the surest way to turn something into a smash is to ban it. That's why I was so grateful that the prison people in Tasmania tried to ban me from writing. Thanks for the extra publicity, fellas.

Like just about everyone else in Victoria at the time, I had got a copy of *Underbelly*, all thirteen episodes, despite its being restricted.

I was pleased to see I made an appearance. A young bloke by the name of Renato Fabretti played me when I was twenty-three. He didn't do a bad job. He did about as good a job as Eric Bana did in *Chopper*.

In the end, Eddie McGuire did a pretty good job too, really. He has made Channel Nine a lot of money. I hope those pinstriped blokes in Sydney are eternally grateful to you, Eddie.

Speaking of football people, Kevin Sheedy, the old Essendon coach who's moved to Sydney, always says, 'History shows we never learn from history.' People in Melbourne certainly didn't learn from history that Mark Read can smell a bloodbath coming from miles away. I wouldn't have survived this long if I couldn't.

I was predicting the Melbourne gangland bloodbath long before it happened. But no one would listen. As the bodies piled up, the police and politicians denied there was a gangland war going on in Melbourne. I wonder what their agenda was!

They finally had to admit it, though, and in 2003 they set up the Purana Task Force. The task force found out what I could have told them anyway – that Carl Williams, after being shot by Jason Moran, wanted just about everyone else in the underworld dead. It was all about greed for drug money, and another instance of drugs having ruined the criminal world.

Back in 1999, I saw it coming, which is why someone called me the Nostradamus of the underworld. Oh yeah, that was me.

That year, I wrote:

Make no mistakes, the bodies will keep falling but for reasons I do not understand no one seems to get excited.

You can find it between the fashion pages and the sports pages.

I was referring here to the death notices in the newspaper. But I've interrupted myself.

They write more about a new risotto recipe than the blood and guts of an underworld war. God help us and pass me a café latte.

Let's make it clear on the long-range forecast. Before this is finished it will make the old Market Murders back in the 1960s look like nude mud wrestling.

There is a group of whackers who ran around flogging, belting and shooting people when they were part of Al's team.

Each and every one of them has been noted and their dance cards have been marked. They will all get a visit and then will head to the morgue.

In years to come, we will talk of the sabre-toothed tiger, the dodo and Alphonse's crew in the same breath . . . all extinct.

I was considering retiring from crime writing but, from what I have heard, I may have a lot more to write about quite soon. There are more bodies to come. As I concluded back in 1999:

If you sit by a river for long enough, you see the bodies of all your enemies float by.

I said that years ago.

I forgot to mention that they will float past a damn sight quicker if you have a couple of mates upstream pushing the bastards in for you.

My first book had a chapter called 'Who's Who in the Zoo', where I listed some of the main players around Pentridge, and a bit about them. This is more like 'Who's Who in the Cemetery'!

It all began in a workmanlike way, if you will excuse the pun, when Alphonse Gangitano shot Gregory John Workman on 7 February 1995. Alphonse got off a homicide charge, but only lasted another three years himself. On 16 January 1998, Alphonse Gangitano departed this mortal coil, probably courtesy of Jason Moran.

Then came the death of John Furlan.

If you think Toyota has been having problems with crook cars, spare a thought for Furlan and his white Subaru Liberty. The brakes didn't just fail, or the cruise control just jam. The bloody thing blew up as he was driving around . . . on 3 August 1998.

He was a used-car dealer, was Johnny Furlan. I've used this line a few times before, but it's one of my favourites, so I hope you don't mind hearing it again: 'He sold bombs and he died in one!'

The next death, that of Mad Charlie Hegyaljie, on 23 November 1998, was a real shock to me.

As I have said, my first son is named after Charlie. We had our differences over the years but, all up, he was a friend of mine for a long, long time. And some of the last words we spoke to each other, just before young Charlie Vincent Read was born, confirmed that friendship.

Then came Vince Mannella, on 9 January 1999, almost a year after the sad passing of Alphonse Gangitano. Mannella thought he was a hot-shot gangster. He wasn't that hot, but he ended up shot.

When he was found dead, his blood-spattered head was lying on the welcome mat of his own house. Someone had been lurking in the bushes.

Joe Quadara died on 28 May 1999, gunned down in a supermarket car park in Toorak. Poor bugger had cancer and was on his way out anyway.

Vicki Jacobs got shot while asleep in her bed alongside her six-year-old son. She was shot for the serious crime of being the wife of a no-hoper by the name of Gerald Preston. It was a weak act, killing her.

The next one on the hit parade was Dimitrios Belias, on 9 September 1999. 'Jimmy the Greek' was found by cleaners outside a St Kilda office. He was one of Mad Charlie's men for a while, and also did some stuff for Alphonse Gangitano.

Towards the end of 1999, the bodies were piling up but still no one seemed to notice all that much. Or if they did, they weren't all that bothered about it.

The next to go was Gerardo Mannella, brother of the dear departed Vince, shot in North Fitzroy on 20 October 1999. Apparently, Gerardo was asking a few too many questions about who shot Vince. Bye bye, Gerardo! Cue Bon Jovi: Shot through the heart and you're to blame.

The next to go was Frank Benvenuto, found shot dead at the wheel of his car on 8 May 2000. Who was to blame? It might have been Andrew 'Benji' Veniamin, or it might have been Mark Moran.

Reshard 'Richard' Mladenich, my old mate from H Division, was the next to get topped, in a St Kilda motel. We were into the noughties by now . . . 16 May 2000.

Someone had been very naughty. King Richard was part of the Morans' set-up, not the sort of existence that would get you discounts on a life insurance policy.

Which brings us to Mark Moran, killed 15 June 2000. 'Marked', he was, probably pretty much from birth. His father was Leslie John Cole, who was shot dead outside his home in Sydney, back in 1982. His mother was Judy Moran. She once turned up on television wearing a T-shirt that read 'I HATE CHOPPER READ'.

That was because she didn't like the fact that I had predicted the death of her other son, Mark's half-brother, Jason Moran, in one of my books. On the back cover of *Chopper 10½* there was a picture of me, shirt off, with a big shovel and looking as handsome as ever alongside three headstones.

On the first headstone were the words 'Mad Charlie' and the date of his death. On the second headstone was 'Big Al' and the date of Alphonse Gangitano's death. And the third headstone just had 'Jason Moran' followed by a question mark.

Mark Moran was one of those people who never seemed to do a day's work but lived in a bloody big house. He had been with his half-brother, Jason, when he shot Carl Williams in the guts.

Dino Dibra was the next to go, killed by Paul Kallipolitis and Benji on 14 October 2000. They were supposed to be his friends.

Friends were also the downfall of George Germanos, on 22 March 2001.

I read recently that Victor Peirce's wife, Wendy, described me as 'a bit of a character, a comedian and a nice man'. Thanks, Wendy. Victor Peirce was one of the people behind the Walsh Street killings. The two young police officers died on 12 October 1998, the day after police shot Graeme Jensen. It was a dog act. Victor had probably lived a charmed life after that. Benji ended it for him on 1 May 2002.

I suppose by now you're wondering who's benefiting from all these murders. Melbourne's funeral directors, that's who.

The next to require the services of the Ladies in White, or Tobin Brothers or whoever, was Paul Kallipolitis. Clock up another one for Benji, 15 October 2002.

And then yet another: Nik 'The Bulgarian' Radev. The getaway car was a Holden Vectra, similar to the one owned by Carl Williams's old man, George Williams. By now it's April 2003 and the whole world is yelling that something is going on in the Melbourne underworld.

And Melbourne's starting to get the sort of bad press around the world that no amount of Formula One races and Commonwealth Games, and all those other big events, can stop. It was turning into the Chicago of the Southern Hemisphere. Except, our Al didn't get done on taxation charges the way Al Capone did. They say that death and taxes are inevitable. Inevitably, our Southern Hemisphere Al got death.

A male prostitute by the name of Shane Chartres-Abbott died next, on 4 June 2003. Who cares?

Then came the big one – Jason Moran. I went back to that picture on the back of *Chopper 10½*, and scratched out the question mark and wrote in 21 June 2003.

I had first heard of Jason Moran from a bloke called Brian Carl Hanson, in 1986. He told me his wife had been bashed by someone of that name at the Chevron in Melbourne. Brian asked me if, when I got out of jail, I would put one up the arse of Jason Moran.

I got out of jail later that year. I was thirty-two and Jason Moran was nineteen. I met up with Jason – Mad Charlie was with me – and did what Hanson asked. I gave him a kick right up the arse.

And then I put a few shots at his feet. That got him dancing pretty nicely.

After I did that, he hopped into his Porsche and drove away. He didn't like me very much after that.

I came across him in Smith Street, Collingwood two weeks before he died. He had a coat on and I was convinced he was wearing a gun. I had a coat on too and he thought I was carrying a gun.

I crossed the street and shook his hand; he was very tentative about putting his hand out. I asked him what he was doing in that neck of the woods. We made some small talk and that was it.

Truth was, I didn't have a gun. Those days were way behind me by then. But I am pretty sure Jason had one on him, and for good reason. In many ways, Jason started it all when he shot Carl Williams in the guts.

He knew Carl was after him, and had been on the move for a while, staying in different houses around the place.

The hit that killed Jason Moran was a very good one, one of the best in the history of hits. He was shot dead along with Pasquale Barbaro, while they sat in his car at a football ground in Essendon. They were watching a game of kids football. Jason's twins, a girl and boy, were also in the car. Victor Brincat, the killer, must have got a bit of blood on the kids, but didn't hurt them.

What Brincat did in pulling off that hit was pretty sensational. He ran 1500 metres with a shotgun and magnum, pulled off the hit, then ran another 1500 metres to get away. He was a vegetarian and fitness fanatic; he should have been in the Olympic pentathlon team.

It took a lot of guts to pull off that hit, but when Brincat got to jail, he lost his guts, and rolled over and dobbed everyone in. It happens to a lot of people when they get into prison. Prison messes with your head. While Brincat had the guts to do the job, he didn't have the guts to do the sentence.

Next to go was Willie Thomson on 21 July 2003. Chalk it up to Carl Williams.

Chalk another one up to Benji Veniamin: Mark Mallia, on 18 August 2003.

A few weeks later, another drug dealer, Housam Zayat, met his maker.

Then it was Michael Ronald Marshall's turn, the hit ordered by Carl Williams at the request of a bloke called Tony Mokbel, the man who had the worst bad hair day in the history of bad hair days.

Victor Brincat was arrested for that murder as well. Again it happened in front of children; again it featured a dash in to do the killing and a dash to a getaway car.

Tony Mokbel cost the Australian taxpayer a lot of money when he was brought back from Greece, where he had escaped to via an elaborate plan involving boats and farmhouses up the country, and all sorts of things he must have thought were pretty clever. And that wig.

Graham 'The Munster' Kinniburgh might have been looking forward to Christmas 2003, but he never got to see it. On 13 December, it was goodnight. His crime was probably being too close to the Morans. He had been at Alphonse's house shortly before Al died, back in 1998. He went out to get some cigarettes and, shortly after, came back to find Alphonse dead on the floor. Up until then, while he was well known in the criminal world, he didn't have much of a profile outside it. That changed. Pretty quickly too, and he was banned from the racetracks around Melbourne and the casino. He was a good mate of Mick Gatto's.

Which brings us to the next death, that of Benji Veniamin, on 23 March 2004. I will deal with this one in detail in the chapter on my good friend Mick Gatto.

There was an unusual story about Benji's death that emerged last year – the vigil that Carl Williams's wife, Roberta, held alongside the body. She also put expensive champagne into his coffin, and warm clothes because she knew he didn't like the cold.

The next death was one that really hit the headlines. Lewis Moran was gunned down in the Brunswick Club, Sydney Road, on 31 March 2004, around the start of the AFL season. Well, poor old Lewis was never going to find out who won the premiership that year.

A lot of people had tried to protect Lewis. But he enjoyed his beer at the Brunswick Club and lots of people knew that. You can't afford to be too predictable in the criminal world.

Lewis Caine was the next to go, on 8 May 2004, though, for the life of me, I don't know why. He was a lightweight, a bloke who I used to kick up the arse in the showers in H Division. He was killed in Brunswick too. Now, there's a place to stay out of.

My old enemy who can't be named is doing time for both those deaths, Lewis Moran and Lewis Caine.

Who shot Terence and Christine Hodson? Well, they 'copped' it on 15 May 2004. Chris Masters devoted a whole *Four Corners* program to Terence and Chris Hodson. Another waste of the taxpayers' money!

In May 2005, a bloke by the name of Lee Patrick Torney disappeared. They found his body down a mine shaft in March 2006.

By now, everyone thought it must be over. All the Morans, bar Judy and her brother-in-law Tuppence, were gone to the great gangland gathering in the sky. Benji had probably gone the other way – to the hell that Wendy Peirce wished he would rot in.

Then, on 6 February 2006, Mario Condello ended up dead, probably the victim of a hit paid for by Carl Williams and Tony Mokbel. Mario was a good friend of Mick Gatto's. About 600 people turned up to his funeral, as a show of strength from the old Carlton Crew.

It should have been all quiet on the western suburbs front by now, but, lo and behold, up popped the Morans again.

Someone shot poor old Desmond 'Tuppence' Moran on 15 June 2009, while he was having his morning tea and biscuits in his favourite restaurant in Ascot Vale. Apparently, his last words were 'Oh shit'.

I got asked to write something in *The Herald Sun* about his death.

Well, 'two-bob' Tuppence Moran is dead. I told friends he'd be dead within the year – and I was right, as I generally am on these matters.

I reckon Tuppence got whacked as general underworld housekeeping.

He was the last one of the Moran crew left and someone's decided to finish them off.

My oath he would have made a few enemies during his life, but this isn't going to re-ignite an underworld war.

Why? Because there's just not enough people to kill. There are only two or three people out there.

Tuppence was the dark horse of the Moran clan. He was the only one with the real criminal power and ability to get things done.

Lewis was a fetch-and-carry boy compared with Tuppence.

Tuppence was the one with the money and the underworld power and authority.

He was the one who could have you shot with a phone call or have you bashed with a nod of his head.

Lewis was just a silly old drunk and a two-bob sneak thief all his life.

He never had any power, any real money, or any authority or any reputation within the criminal world.

Tuppence was regarded as the biggest SP bookmaker in Melbourne, taking bets over the phone from a prominent politician and business tycoon who will remain nameless.

It was rumoured the late Kane brothers used to work for Tuppence as collectors – working on a 50-50 cut for large outstanding debts.

A $10,000 debt would be split 50-50 – half for Tuppence and half for the Kanes.

But thrifty Tuppence wasn't as generous with his own clan.

Nephew Jason worked for Tuppence as a collector for a 25 percent cut.

It is said no one ever got a 50-50 deal out of Tuppence after the Kanes died.

I don't mourn his passing.

He didn't like me, and I didn't like him – end of story.

His passing brings to an end a criminal dynasty. Good riddance.

The same day that article appeared, Judy Moran appeared in court, charged with being an accessory to the murder of Tuppence Moran. Another sister-in-law, Suzanne Kane, was also charged with being an accessory. Suzanne Kane's de facto, Geoffrey 'Nuts' Armour, has been charged with the murder, along with Michael Farrugia. After that, it all became *sub judice*, or sub Judyce! Ha ha!

There were times in the past when, even though I knew she didn't like me, I could have felt sorry for Judy Moran. She had lost two husbands and two sons to gangland murders.

A world-famous jailbird by the name of Oscar Wilde once said something about how to lose one parent is unfortunate, to lose two is careless. See, a lot of jailbirds end up as famous authors. Maybe I should write 'The Ballad of Pentridge Jail'.

Anyway, as much as I tried to have sympathy for Judy Moran over the years, there was always something about her not to like. It was sort of reconfirmed with the death of Tuppence.

According to the evidence at her bail hearing, when the coppers came to arrest her, she told them she couldn't leave until she had spoken to Lewis. She went into another room in the house, where his ashes were kept in a large urn, and said, 'I am sorry, Lew.'

I was only just getting over all that when, one sunny day in April of this year, came news that made me laugh out loud. Carl Williams had been bashed to death in the high-security Acacia unit at Barwon Prison.

When they built the new Barwon Prison near Geelong, they didn't make the same mistake they did with Jika Jika, by giving it an Aboriginal name. This time, they named the units after native plants. They have so many precious petals there, I suppose.

The prison is split into many separate units. Acacia is, allegedly, high security. Then comes Banksia, which is also for prisoners who need supervision or protection. Hoya is another protection unit, while Cassia gets all the new prisoners. Then you have Diosma, which is for the prison workers; and Eucalypt, for long-term prisoners who aren't in any danger. In 2003, they opened Grevillea, which is for maximum-security prisoners.

But back to that other precious little flower, Carl Williams. Yes, I spat out my drink and laughed my head off, and I thought to myself, 'Hah hah hah, another one bites the dust.'

I knew that Carl would end up getting it sooner or later, and I wasn't surprised that the person who did it might have been an ally of his. I've always said that if someone's going to kill you, it's more likely to be one of your friends or a relative. And it can be done just as easily in prison as outside it. You just have to have the nodding agreement of one of the screws, and rock'n'roll – that's it.

I've never had a very high opinion of Carl Williams. As I said on the day of his death, 'He was just a big, fat, wobbly bottomed kid from Footscray. He wasn't much of a man at all. He was nothing.'

I was asked in April 2010 if I thought that the killing of Carl Williams would lead to more deaths. I said then, and I still believe it, that that would not happen unless someone knocked off his wife, Roberta.

After all, there aren't too many people left to kill. There's only Mick Gatto and me left, really. And no one's going to kill Mick Gatto. He's far too popular.

There was a lot of talk around the time of Carl Williams's death about him becoming a Crown witness, and about corrupt police and so on. It will be interesting to see where all that goes. The day he got killed, there was a story in the paper saying the police were helping pay his daughter's school fees. And there was a lot of speculation about him doing a deal with the police that would have halved his sentences. Obviously, someone didn't think too highly of that arrangement.

I guess, with Carl gone to the great drug factory in the sky, the question is, will another *Underbelly*-style spate of gangland killings happen?

Well, not for a while. As I said, there are not a lot of people left to shoot.

But I've always reckoned these things go in cycles. About once every ten years, these things erupt.

Greed and drugs, and a bunch of coppers who won't listen to the warnings from an old man by the name of Mark Brandon 'Chopper' Read, will probably see it all repeated around 2020.

You read it here first!

CHAPTER 12

A GENTLEMAN FROM THE OLD SCHOOL – MICK GATTO

I get three mentions in Mick Gatto's book and they are all favourable. And I am pleased to see that his book is doing okay out there in the marketplace, because I've discovered Mick Gatto to be a pretty decent, honourable man.

Mick and I have lunch together and talk about all sorts of things. It's probably strange that we have ended up mates, since he was so close to Alphonse Gangitano.

Mick is a former Victorian heavyweight boxing champion who was also a heavyweight in the illegal gambling scene around Melbourne. The word was that, for a time, he was one of Alphonse's business partners. That was what I was led to believe, anyway, and the politics of the underworld being what they are, there are certain people you just don't meet up with.

Alphonse was the Carlton mafia crime boss – the Plastic Godfather, I used to call him – and Mick was supposed to be sort of his second-string man. That's how the police saw it and that's how the media saw it. Even my crazy mate Mad Charlie thought this to be the truth, and Charlie considered himself to be the absolute crime authority.

The whisper was that Mick was this quiet voice always trying to inject a word of sanity into what was becoming a pretty insane world, the one of Alphonse Gangitano. After the King Street nightclub attack, Jason Moran apparently said of Alphonse, 'He's a fucking lulu. If you smash five pool cues and an iron bar over someone's head, you're a fucking lulu.' When your friends are calling you a lulu, I guess you must be a lulu.

Alphonse was probably just living up to his name. The name 'Alphonse' comes from an old German word meaning 'always ready for battle'.

I suppose I had always liked Mick Gatto because of what I had heard about him from a distance. I doubted we would ever become mates, though, and sit down and break bread together, even if a lot of water has gone under the bridge since the early Carlton Crew days.

However, through Dave Hedgcock, who is also a really good friend of mine, I was able to meet Mick. Dave runs a mediation service in Melbourne and is a good mate of Mick's. It's amazing the amount of respect there is for Dave around Melbourne. When he sits down at a dispute, he just has an amazing ability to get people to start speaking to each other.

Dave must have spoken up for me with Mick. That's how it happens in the criminal world: if someone, particularly someone like Dave Hedgcock, speaks up for you, then other people might start to think you're not such a bad bloke after all. And it eventually led to us getting together.

It really started one day when I rang Dave Hedgcock to see if he could get me some 'ungettable' tickets to see the Rolling Stones at Rod Laver Arena in Melbourne the last time they were in Australia.

I love the Rolling Stones. I don't have a favourite song of theirs, really, but Margaret reckons her favourite is 'You Can't Always Get What You Want'. Sums things up a bit, I suppose. Keith Richards is my favourite Rolling Stone. He's a real survivor.

I don't mind a good concert. As I mentioned, I went to see AC/DC when they were in Melbourne in 2010, and Jimmy Barnes always has me backstage when he plays in Melbourne. He even featured me in one of his DVDs, in the song 'Sit on My Knee'.

Anyway, I asked Dave to see if he could get me these Rolling Stones tickets. It seems he had a direct line to Paul Dainty, the famous promoter, and, the next thing you know, Margaret and I had two tickets right up close to the stage. We could see all of Mick Jagger's wrinkles without having to look at the big screen. Margaret reckoned that Mick Jagger looked like one of those Shar Pei dogs. And when we sat down, guess who was sitting right in front of us?

Eddie McGuire and his wife. It is true, Eddie is everywhere.

After the concert, I was told that Mick Gatto had also had a hand in me getting the tickets to see Mick Jagger and the boys. To thank him for his kindness, I invited Dave over to the art gallery where all my paintings were on display, and told Dave to grab a painting for himself, and to take one for Mick Gatto too.

Dave picked for Mick a brightly coloured painting of Ned Kelly boxing. It was a pretty bad painting. Dave rang Mick Gatto to tell him he had chosen this painting of mine for him. He then handed the phone to me.

I said to Mick Gatto, 'Thanks for the tickets, mate. And don't judge me too harshly by the artwork.'

He laughed and said thanks.

I am told he has the painting hanging in his gym. I feel quite honoured by that. And also by the fact he mentioned me in his book three times and didn't say a bad word about me.

That put to bed a lot of misunderstandings I had about the bloke because of his previous associates. Mick Gatto is, I have since found, a gentleman from the old school. I consider him to be a long, long way from the underworld-crime figure the newspapers depict him as, as do some other crime books and television programs. I would consider him to be a former heavyweight boxer and bouncer, who also worked in the Victoria Markets with his father, then developed, along with Nappy Ollington, what is now a past interest in Melbourne's illegal gambling industry.

Mick was supposed to have heavied a few people from time to time for moneys he was owed. I don't reckon he would have had to heavy them too much. He's a pretty imposing sort of figure.

Nappy Ollington, by the way, ran a floating two-up school in Melbourne's western and northern suburbs for years. He was a great campaigner for having the game legalised and was eventually invited by Crown Casino to help set up their legal two-up school.

I reckon we can now consider both these men as dinky-di Australian legends, who are right up there with RM Williams and Slim Dusty. Mick Gatto has certainly gone way beyond the Italian-wog-hood-gangster image the media created for him. In its rush to destroy him, the media has done what the American media did with Wild Bill Hickok – turned Mick Gatto into a national legend.

It's the same thing they've done with a bloke by the name of Chopper Read and also Roger 'The Dodger' Rogerson, and a few others I just can't manage to remember right now. Ha ha.

I learned a long time ago never to believe all the stuff you read in the media. I used to read a lot of stuff about me that wasn't true, so I was pretty sure a lot of what they were saying about Mick would have been made up. One hundred facts and 1000 fairytales.

So, anyway, Mick, thanks for the tickets to the Rolling Stones. And to the boxing match at the Docklands. And for the best wishes when my DVD *Fatbelly* came out last year. That was a nice gesture.

I am always looking forward to our next lunch. A few more ears burning around town, eh? Those who have got ears, that is. I really enjoy our chats, talking about jail and some of the things that went on there and, of course, mutual friends and mutual enemies. It seems we have a lot of both in common.

But, funnily, Mick doesn't remember an incident that has left me with a big dent in my head; just one of my many scars. When I was nineteen I went to the Myer Music Bowl in Melbourne, to a big Sharpies' dance. When I walked behind a curtain near the stage, someone whacked me in the head with a claw hammer. Then this big bloke came and rescued me, and put me in a taxi and sent me off to St Vincent's Hospital. I remember waking up there, with this jelly-like stuff on the pillow. A bit of skull the size of a sixpence came out, and I pushed it back in.

Anyway, yet again, I had survived and I asked, 'Who helped me out?'

I was told it was Mick Gatto, who was working there as a bouncer that night. I've thanked him before in one of my books but he says he can't remember that night, or helping me out.

We have something else in common. Mick Gatto knows well the value of having a lawyer of the highest calibre; in his case, literally. Michael Hodgman QC MP was the big shot who hugely boosted my chances of getting out of jail in Tasmania. In the case of the shooting of Sammy the Turk, for me, it was Pat Harvey and the two barristers he got on board. For Mick, it was the Melbourne barrister Robert Richter QC. I made that pun about him being of the highest calibre because his knowledge of guns helped get Mick acquitted of the murder of gangland killer Andrew 'Benji' Veniamin. Richter was able to prove that Mick was acting in self-defence because one of the bullets misfired, because both men were grappling over the gun. The jury took just one day to find Mick not guilty.

Robert Richter QC said the police should have worked out a lot earlier that Mick was not guilty but, and I like this line, they didn't 'because people were acting on a presumption of guilt, not a presumption of innocence'. Mick's line after finally getting out of jail after fourteen months was pretty good too: 'Thank God for the jury system and thank God for Robert Richter, a top barrister.'

That's another thing Mick and I can talk about, that lovely feeling you get when you hear a jury say the words 'Not guilty'.

CHAPTER 13

ELLE, KERRI-ANNE, ALAN AND ME!

Chopper drunk on McFeast
by Halliwell Hannah

The debut of *Elle McFeast Live* (16/3) on the ABC got off to a controversial start when Elle McFeast's first guest appeared on the show drunk.

Mark 'Chopper' Read, an infamous criminal and author of about seven books on the Australian crime scene, appeared bleary eyed and spoke with a slur.

The glare of television lights seemed to bother him as he struggled to answer McFeast's questions about toe-cutting and other sordid criminal activities.

Finally he admitted the obvious and slurred . . .

'You've had me stuck in your b$##@% Green Room drinking Melbourne Bitter. I've just done six cans. Then you bring me on as p%$$#@ as a parrot and ask me in-depth questions. I'm obviously drunk. I'm no use to anybody. It's not fair'.

At one stage he took out his false teeth and announced with pride . . .

'These are the James Bond, the carte blanche, the Rolls Royce of false teeth and I'd like you to pay some form of b$##@% respect to these false teeth.'

After ogling McFeast's cleavage and mumbling some incoherent answers, the Earless One was led off to a corner of the set by the cheeky host, and left there to quietly booze on for the remainder of the show.

That's how Melbourne's *Herald Sun* reported my infamous appearance on Elle McFeast's program on 16 March 1998.

About eight weeks after I had got out of Risdon Prison, I got a call from the ABC, wanting me to appear on *Elle McFeast Live*. Apparently, her mother had insisted she talk to me. Elle (Libbi Gorr) asked her whom she would like to see interviewed and she said 'Chopper Read'. She also said I was the Quentin Tarantino of Australian authors and that she liked my books.

I had to fly from Hobart to Sydney, to do the interview at the ABC studio at Gore Hill. Funny that – Elle McFeast's real name is Libbi Gorr but I don't think that hill was named after her. There's a pretty famous cemetery at Gore Hill, though; her live television career might be buried there.

At the time I made the trip, I was on Xanax, a very powerful anti-anxiety drug. The instructions on the bottle say not to take it with alcohol.

I had taken twelve milligrams of Xanax, and had been drinking at Hobart airport and then on the plane. I had to change planes at Melbourne before getting a connecting flight to Sydney. So I had a few more drinks in Melbourne. And a few more on the plane as it headed towards Sydney.

Then I had a few more drinks while I was waiting for the people from the McFeast show to arrive. Well, you do, don't you? They showed up, including these two gay bodyguards. They were huge but very light on their tootsies and giggling all over the place. They were quite happy to see me; I was pretty fit back then.

I got to the ABC studio and Elle's offsider took over looking after me from there. She took me to the green room and showed me a fridge full of Melbourne Bitter beer. She said, 'You don't go on for two hours.'

I said, 'Well, what do I do in the meantime?'

I started drinking and got drunker.

Little Tina Arena, who was going to be on the same show, saw me and asked, 'Are you all right to go on TV?'

I was quite pissed and put my arm around her. I said, 'Do you mind me saying this? You've got big tits on TV, but you're just a tiny little thing.'

And she is, she's just under five feet tall. She said the reason she looked like she had big tits on TV was that she had a narrow back. Funny, isn't it, how you remember these things? Anyway, after that conversation,

I had fallen asleep on the floor in front of the fridge, and the two big gay bouncers had to come and pick me up.

Meanwhile, Tina Arena had gone to Elle and said, 'You can't have Chopper on, he's blind drunk.'

Elle said, 'No, he's coming on, it would be good television.'

So, bear in mind, she was warned.

They pushed me out the doorway into the TV studio in front of the cameras. Elle McFeast started asking me questions and, well, Australia knows the rest.

Seemingly, the whole country saw what happened, and it's still up on YouTube.

I made an idiot of myself and Elle McFeast never did a successful live TV show again. They do let her do live radio on the ABC sometimes. I must give her a call when she does talkback. I reckon the seven-second delay button will be pushed the moment I say, 'G'day, Libbi, it's Mark Read.'

I actually saw Libbi Gorr at Tullamarine one day, and she came up to me with tears in her eyes. She put her arms around me and said she was so glad she had met me again because it would allow her to have closure.

She said, 'You know you destroyed my TV career.'

I said, 'No, you destroyed your TV career when you insisted on having a drunk Chopper Read on TV. So don't go blaming me.'

All hell had broken loose after my appearance on *McFeast*.

The Federal Minister for Communications, Senator Richard Alston, went ballistic. He had his riding instructions from Johnny Howard to kick the shit out of the ABC every chance he got. He didn't need a free kick like the one Elle McFeast gave him. For him, this was a golden opportunity. He said he was appalled and that my TV appearance offended community standards and so on. He also said it showed a lack of editorial control and that it was his understanding that the ABC regretted it. Obviously, Elle McFeast does.

It seems that at the time, though, she and her producers tried to claim I was putting on an act. I wasn't – I was pissed to the eyeballs.

As I said at the time, I think that when they had this big bloke with gold teeth and no ears in their green room, the ABC staff were too frightened to stop me from drinking.

Jeff Kennett, the premier of Victoria, also entered the fray, and was kind of on my side. He said that I should never have been asked onto the show by the ABC and that, as a person just out of jail, I should have been getting help to reintegrate into the community, not being put on live television.

The whole issue just blew up terribly. It was featured on *Media Watch*. I find myself in all sorts of strange places sometimes; Chopper Read on *Media Watch* – who would ever have thought of that? It probably came about because, in addition to the McFeast appearance, a few days later Channel Nine had got me on *The Midday Show* with Kerri-Anne Kennerley.

This is what Kerri-Anne said: 'We've decided not to go ahead with the interview with Chopper Read live on this program.

'I guess it is what you would call a value judgement but we took the high moral ground and there was a lot of heated debate about it.

'We might be wrong but the question remains, I think, the question to be asked is should a convicted killer and torturer be given publicity or not?

'To discuss the issue, we welcome broadcaster Alan Jones.'

Well, for a start, Kerri-Anne, I am not a convicted killer. She got that wrong, and it was only going to get a damn sight worse for Kerri-Anne.

Channel Nine hadn't decided not to do the live interview with Chopper Read. Oh no, sirree.

They had arranged for me to be driven from Glen Air, where I was living with Mary-Ann, to WIN studios in the suburb of New Town in Hobart, about a half-hour trip. When I got to the studios, they locked me in the green room and removed all the beer. They sat me by the telephone and told me to ring the number of the Channel Nine studios in Sydney.

I rang the number. Whoever answered told me to hold on.

I was looking at the TV and Alan Jones was on and he was really getting stuck into me.

'Well, it could only happen on the ABC and taxpayers fund that sort of stuff,' he said. 'And I think that responsible and decent Australians who are taxpayers find that whole treatment absolutely horrific and appalling.'

Then someone said, 'Go ahead, Chopper.'

I said, 'Chopper Read here,' and they could hear me on the loudspeaker in the studios in Sydney.

Kerri-Anne asked Alan Jones if he wanted to take the call. He said, 'It is your program, Kerri-Anne.' He was disappointed I had rung up.

She said to the crowd, 'Do you want him to speak to Chopper Read?' And they said yes.

Alan Jones started really bagging me again.

I told him that a bloke who lives in a glass house shouldn't throw stones.

He asked me what I was talking about.

I said that I never got arrested in a public toilet in London.

Kerri-Anne jumped up and down about ending the interview there and then, and they went to an ad break very quickly. When they returned, Alan still had not regained his composure.

Since then I have read Chris Masters's book on Alan Jones, *Jonestown*. As a result, I have had to reassess Alan. I know Chris tried to put shit on him, but I think did the opposite. I have never been a great fan of Chris Masters, having met him once myself. I reckon that anyone Chris Masters dislikes enough to write a book like that about can't be all that bad.

Then I looked at all of Alan Jones's achievements, considering the rough start he had in life. He had come off a farm somewhere in the Queensland outback. He was a pretty good tennis player, apparently, and a pretty bright student. Alan became a schoolteacher, then wrote speeches for Malcolm Fraser, the Liberal prime minister. He's supposed to be the one who came up with the line 'Life isn't meant to be easy'. Alan could have written that for me.

Then he became a rugby coach. He ended up coaching Australia, and they won a Grand Slam and beat New Zealand. And he did this even though he never played the game. It seems he was a great speaker, a great motivator. He has been an adviser to kings and billionaires, and he rules Sydney radio and is a very powerful man in that city.

So, I said to myself, 'Who cares if he is or isn't as camp as a row of tents, it is none of my business.' I get a funny feeling he is more of an asexual person, anyway.

I wrote him a letter, care of the publishers of the Chris Masters book; I said I wanted him to accept my apologies for what I said on Kerri-Anne's show, and said I had no right or business to hit below the belt like that. It was heartfelt and I hope that if he didn't get that letter, that at least he reads this and does accept my apologies.

I believe Alan Jones has never mentioned my name on radio or TV or in print ever since. I must tune in to the ABC sometime to see if Libbi Gorr ever gives me a mention. After all, we both barrack for Collingwood!

CHAPTER 14

THE WEDDING

I proposed to Margaret on the Channel Ten news. But I am the first to admit I am not the greatest romantic in the world. I am not really a flowers-and-chocolates sort of person. So, in many ways, the wedding was very much Margaret's project, and she pulled it off beautifully.

In honour of my father, who had fought with the Gordon Highlanders, I wore a kilt. Since I'm sure you asked the obvious next question, I wore red underpants underneath it. I had to keep pulling up the kilt to show off these red underpants because everyone wanted to know what I had on under the kilt.

As for all the other things that happened at our wedding, and there were plenty, I will let Margaret tell the rest of the story. It was her planning that really made the day go like clockwork.

Her careful attention to the smallest detail when it came to the seating arrangements – something that, when you look at the guest list, was mandatory – needs to be appreciated too.

MARGARET: I had no idea Mark was going to marry me when he returned from Tasmania. I was just happy to have him back.

Even when we were separated by so many different things – his first marriage, Risdon Prison, Bass Strait – I think I knew in my heart that we would somehow end up together again. Our wedding, on 19 January 2003, was the pathway to a whole new beginning for both of us.

We had agreed to take different paths in Tasmania, as I couldn't cope with the severity of his last prison sentence. I just could not stay either in Tasmania or in a relationship with him after he was sentenced. And, anyway, the Tasmanian police were making it pretty clear they didn't want me around.

When he came back to Melbourne, I laid things out for Mark very clearly. He had to choose between a life with me or his old ways in the underworld. 'If you want to stay in that lifestyle, you can forget about us,' I told him. He chose me.

He began to change in many other ways too. He was well known as an author, and as the subject of the film *Chopper*. So, he of course got onto the public-speaking circuit, teaming up with Mark 'Jacko' Jackson. Mark Jackson is a very, very funny man. He is most famous in football for standing on his head in the middle of a game after kicking five goals. Why did he do that? Because a member of the opposition had told him he would never kick five goals while ever his backside pointed to the ground.

So, a new Mark Read was emerging who I felt very comfortable about living the rest of my life with.

We were married at Banksia Court, Ivanhoe – the most wonderful of settings, just perfect. It is a beautiful old mansion. The original owner was the founder of the Eye and Ear Hospital in East Melbourne. The day matched the setting – it was perfect too.

The array of guests – 127 people – was certainly a mixed bag. Because of that mixture of people, I would describe our wedding as wacky, but everyone had a wow of a time.

I had no idea Mark was going to turn up in a kilt. I've got to say, he looked absolutely fantastic, but, gee whoever would have thought that Mark Read would wear a skirt, let alone get married in one? It still makes me laugh. But it shows again how much Mark likes to make a big statement.

I was in much more traditional dress: an off-white satin off-the-shoulder gown, with a beaded bodice, train and lace-bordered skirt, completed with a white veil. I also wore a beautiful glass necklace I'd borrowed from Gloria, a friend of twenty years, and which she had worn when she got married. It was a wonderful gift, for which I will forever be grateful.

We had people from the media there, including journalists from Channel 7, Channel Nine and Channel Ten. Andrew Rule and John Silvester, Mark's original publishers, were there too, as were some lawyers. Also present were prison guards from Mark's time in Pentridge; people who had befriended me also and helped both of us through some of the most difficult times.

They had the most wonderful little gift for us, his and hers Ku Klux Klan hoods.

That was a reminder of the picture that appeared in Mark's first book of him with prison guard Peter Prideaux and Brian Furlong. Mark was standing between the two of them wearing a Ku Klux Klan hood. It was all a bit of a joke, a way of killing time in prison. Mark called himself the hood in the hood.

Anyway, we both have hoods now. It always makes me laugh when I bring them out.

What a thoughtful gift.

Our MC, Rob Porter, was formerly a sergeant in the armed robbery squad. He congratulated us on committing to the wonderful institution of marriage, adding that I was very lucky because Mark was already an expert on institutions. Mark 'Jacko' Jackson gave me away.

One of Mark's best friends, the Archibald Prize–winning painter Adam Cullen, was there, but none of the Reads made it to the wedding. The only member of my family there was my brother Ron. Still, Joe 'The Boss' Ditroia absconded from parole in Adelaide just to attend the wedding.

Joe's speech was very moving. He talked about how he regarded Mark as his big brother because of all the things they had shared. He said that anyone who has done time in prison would know how hard it is to make friends there but that he really regarded Mark as a good friend. He also talked about how he admired the way I had kept visiting Mark while he was in Pentridge.

Sammy Hutchinson was there too. He was an old-time bank robber who served a long stretch with Mark in

H Division. When Sammy gave his speech he had us all in stitches.

Sammy lamented all the changes at Pentridge now that it was no longer a prison. He said if he tried to escape from C Division now he would end up in someone's carefully manicured backyard. And Sammy is well qualified to talk about escaping. He made many attempts from Pentridge, using his faithful homemade rope and grappling hook. 'I lived there for twenty years and loved it. It's sad to see an old friend like H Division mistreated,' he said.

Sammy got a standing ovation but Mark thought the time had come to move him along. He gave him a kiss and gently removed him from the podium.

Mark's best man, Richard Levan, also spoke, saying that Mark had been very kind to the Albanian community. Richard is the son of the late Norm Dardovski, head of one of the largest and most powerful Albanian families in Melbourne.

Then, Adam Cullen, wearing a Cameron Highlander kilt, decided he wanted to speak. He was as drunk as a lord and grabbed the microphone to deliver the most insane speech of the night. He declared Mark Brandon Chopper Read to be not a criminal but a cross between Ned Kelly and Henry Lawson. He threw the microphone down and staggered back to his chair, only to return to the stage to declare he had nothing more to say on the matter.

Jimmy Barnes couldn't make the wedding, but we had a covers band, and the singer looked just like Jimmy. In fact, a lot of people thought that I had pulled it off – Jimmy Barnes singing at the wedding of Mark Read and Margaret Cassar.

Our security was provided by two Albanian brothers who Mark called Anger and Sorrow. They had two hand guns each, which I saw protruding from the shoulder holsters they wore over their shirts. It was a hot evening, so they had taken their jackets off. Outside were ten Albanian guards patrolling the grounds, just to keep the stickybeaks and assorted other intruders away. I don't think a bride has ever felt safer at her wedding.

There were plenty of other memorable moments. Darren Lunny, a Channel Ten news reporter, was dancing with Helen Stefanidis. She's an old friend of Mark's. He met her when he was nineteen and she was fourteen. She's a bleach-blonde woman who was very, very attractive when she was younger. Mark tells a funny story about Helen and a hand gun she took out of her bag when they were having a drink in the Leinster Arms, the pub in Collingwood, just before the wedding. It surprised Mark because he never knew that you could get a .32 calibre magnum hand gun.

Anyway, after the wedding, we found out that Helen had been running around sticking up 7/11 stores and using a taxi as a getaway car. We found out because shortly after our wedding Darren Lunny was on television reporting that this woman had been arrested for carrying out armed robberies using a .32 magnum hand gun and using a taxi as a getaway car.

But even though he was there at the scene when they arrested Helen, he had no idea that it was the woman with bleach-blonde hair he had been dancing with at our wedding. Mark tried to ring him up shortly afterwards and let him know, but he didn't get through. So if he's reading this, the penny will probably drop. Mark still can't believe Darren couldn't have recognised her after dancing with her at our wedding.

With escaped prisoners, former armed robbers and armed robbery squad police, serving police (who we can't name), drunken painters and Albanian bodyguards with guns all present, you can see that it was some wedding.

When Adam's speech (or speeches) was over, it was time for the bridal waltz, to 'The Wonder of You'. Mark is always keen to point out that we also danced to the theme from *The Godfather*.

While there were a lot of memorable speeches that night, the one that really stands out for me is Mark's.

'I've known Margaret for near 30 years,' he said. 'I planned on marrying her a year after I met her, but things kept getting in the way.'

'I had a career to pursue.'

That got a laugh. He joked about other people going off to study to be lawyers, architects and engineers while he went to Bible College, but that he reckoned he had ended up doing better than everyone else.

Then he got serious. 'I'd like to thank Margaret for marrying me,' he said. He then beautifully summed it all up for both of us: 'This is a victory for Margaret and me, for what we have been through; this is a victory.'

He was right; we had accomplished something very special that day. It was the storybook ending to a friendship that began in the 1970s, a romance that started in the 1980s, and a second chance that began in the twenty-first century, when a plane that had travelled from Hobart landed at Tullamarine airport.

At times it can still be a battle, but that only makes the victories sweeter.

CHAPTER 15

OFF THE RAILS – AGAIN

All my life I've been in trouble of one sort or another, and, from the age of fifteen, I have been on some form of medication or another – I was always wrongfully diagnosed and placed on the incorrect drugs. All this created – or, at least, helped to create – a monster during my teenage years; a monster that lasted all through my twenties and thirties.

Eventually, I overcame my dependence on the highly addictive drug Xanax.

For a while, things went along reasonably well. I worked hard to follow Margaret's rule that I had to make an honest living. However, as I've mentioned, I managed to get myself mixed up with a lot of people who played around with my mental and financial well-being. I can admit now that that caused me to lose the plot. I won't go into all the details, but a couple of years ago I went completely off the rails. I now believe I had a nervous breakdown.

Enter Margaret, to pick up the pieces again. Margaret has a doctor, Helen Kouzmin, who is as much a friend as a doctor to her. When Margaret went to Dr Kouzmin after I had my breakdown, she could see that Margaret was upset. She encouraged Margaret to tell her what was troubling her. Margaret told her she really feared for the future of our marriage.

Dr Kouzmin recommended that I see her husband, pharmacist David Nolte, and also see a psychiatrist by the name of Dr William H Orchard. Dr Bill Orchard is eighty and has been a psychiatrist for nearly fifty years, and is a very intelligent man. He was a Fulbright scholar, and studied to be a psychiatrist in the US and England. He was also a pretty good athlete in his early days, twice representing Australia in water polo at the Olympics: in 1952, in Helsinki; and in 1956, in Melbourne.

Dr Orchard has been a great reformer in the area of psychiatric treatment in hospitals. He wasn't much of a fan of the Howard government, writing that the curtailing of psychotherapy under the national health system was 'the most destructive act perpetrated against the welfare of the mentally ill by a federal government since Federation; an astonishing witch-hunt oppressing both the profession of psychoanalysis, and intellectual life in Australia'.

It was a big thing for me to go and see Dr Bill Orchard. I used to hang shit on psychiatrists. I have still got psychiatrists' reports from my days in prison. They would write page after page after page of pure rubbish. I think that most psychiatrists have an uncontrollable urge to be the next Leo Tolstoy. Bill Orchard likes to write a lot too, but what he writes makes a lot of sense.

Dr Orchard diagnosed me as suffering from ADD – Attention-Deficit Disorder. ADD Type 4 is the most accurate description of what I have, I believe.

Dr Orchard prescribed for me a dose of 500 milligrams of Epilim four times a day. Epilim is a mood stabiliser. He also prescribed five to ten milligrams of dexamphetamine, a stimulant. David Nolte fills these prescriptions for me.

David has worked to help a lot of people overcome serious mental issues, including, I believe, Lester Ellis, the former boxer. He was drinking slabs of beer a day before he got help from David. I know David also believes he can help the AFL footballer Ben Cousins.

Together, Dr Orchard, Dr Kouzmin and David Nolte have really helped me. Instead of flying around the room and staying awake for days on end, like a normal person would do if they took the amount of dexamphetamine a day that I do, I sleep like a log. When I wake, I feel greatly refreshed, and have never felt so sane in my life. I no longer have surges of anger – mental or emotional rages – boiling over in me.

I can only wonder how many of my fellow inmates and all the criminals I have dealt with over the years have also suffered from ADD. And I wonder if they could be helped in the same way that Dr Orchard and David Nolte have helped me. The really sad part is that the government is trying to put Dr Bill Orchard out of business because they disagree with his use of dexamphetamine to treat ADD.

I'm not a medical expert, but I do know that Dr Orchard has been a lifesaver as far as I am concerned, and I don't say that lightly.

I truly believe he pulled me back from suicide, as that is where my mind was heading a couple of years ago, as I struggled to cope with people ripping me off. Had it not been for this doctor and being, finally, correctly diagnosed as suffering from ADD Type 4, I might not be here, scribbling away on my faithful A4 paper.

Anyway, enough of my mental and emotional problems. I've got a future to think about – a bright and happy one that includes enjoying the company of my wife, my sons and now, again thanks to Margaret, my mother.

Thank God for Margaret, hey?

I GET asked a lot if I have any regrets about my life. Nah, I don't regret much at all. Throughout my life, I was confronted with certain situations and dealt with them the way I thought I had to deal with them at the time. End of story.

What would be the good in regretting any of it now, anyway? Would it unburn the feet of all those people? Would it return to their original dimensions the shoe sizes of some of those drug dealers who were a bit slow handing over some of their ill-gotten gains? Would it unshoot the people I shot? No, it wouldn't.

As I have always said, what happened back then just happened. It was just the way I was living my life. And now I am living a different sort of life.

If my mother did curse me at birth – and I am not so sure about that anymore – I have been blessed that I found Margaret Cassar. As I have said throughout this book, I love her.

And I love her even though, at times, she can be very bad tempered. That's the Maltese in her, I suppose, though, from time to time, it might just have been because I haven't been on my best behaviour. The other thing that gets her temper up is when people try to rip me off. These days, people say that to earn my trust, you first have to earn Margaret's. If you get cream biscuits with your cup of tea when you come to our house in Collingwood, you know you're in her good books.

As you've read, Margaret has certainly been a big positive influence on my life, especially since I moved back from Tasmania and we got married; and particularly since she opened up to Dr Helen Kouzmin about my problems, and brought Dr William H. Orchard and David Nolte into our lives. Before that, though, and more than a few times, it was a bugger of an existence for her.

With Dr Orchard's help, with Margaret's support and with the love of a cheeky little bloke who calls me Dad, I feel a lot more in control of my life. Well, I had control of my life before, when I was in prison, but it's a different sort of control now.

We have a pretty ordinary sort of life. We don't go out a lot. We watch a lot of television. We like to go away on holidays. I still do a lot of work, making an honest living on the public-speaking circuit. When I am not working, I like a real lot of sleep. I can, and do, fall asleep just about anywhere. I recently slept through a court appearance for a minor traffic offence.

A few other things have happened that have changed me a fair bit from the person I was back in the 1960s, 70s and 80s. When I saw Mary-Ann give birth to little Charlie, twelve years ago, it was just the most amazing feeling. For the first time in my life, I felt like a member of the human race.

I thought to myself, 'I have just seen a woman give birth to my son, my son.

'Chopper Read has a son.'

When I held little Charlie in my hands, it was just wonderful, wonderful, wonderful!

But it also made me feel vulnerable. I felt vulnerable because people could now hurt me through my son. I have advised a lot of people in the criminal world that family, kids, would be the death of them because that was how their enemies could get to them.

As I wrote in my first book, I had always felt impregnable before because of my lack of family commitments. A few people tried to get at me through my dad, but Keith Alfred Read was big enough to hold his own. As for me, people could do whatever they wanted to me and I never worried about it. They could hit me with a claw hammer or an iron bar, stab with me a screwdriver or shoot me, but it never worried me. It was all part of the challenge – to show no pain, to come back at them bigger and stronger.

But now they could hurt me by hurting someone else – my son. When I saw my second son – Roy Brandon Read – born to Margaret Cassar, via a caesarean, that made me feel twice the human being I had but also twice as vulnerable.

He's a beauty, too, is Roy. He's into little athletics and wants to play cricket. Roy is a good runner, just like his great-grandfather on my mum's side, who had a silver terrine presented to him by King Edward VIII, the bloke who abdicated to marry an American woman, Mrs Simpson.

Straight after he was born, Margaret said she wanted to call our son Brandon but I didn't want to do that. I have always believed it is the height of arrogance to give your child the same name you have.

Margaret loves to tell the story of how I scolded her for calling him Brandon Roy Read as she was being stitched up after the caesarean.

I remember saying to her, 'Well, you really stuffed that up.'

For twenty-four hours, he was known as Brandon Roy Read, but then I got it changed to Roy Brandon Read. I have always liked the name Roy, probably because I was such a big fan of Roy Rogers. And Roy Read had a nice ring to it.

Brandon as a second name has become a bit of a family tradition. It's one that my mother started, bless her.

My sister's son is Jethro Brandon, and her grandson is Kahn Brandon. Jethro Brandon is an accomplished composer. He wrote the music for the film *Van Diemen's Land*.

All up, I would have to say that fatherhood has had a mellowing effect on me. As I said all those years ago in that interview with Diane O'Connor when I was in Jika Jika, I never saw myself as the doting parent with a brood of kids. I don't have a brood, I suppose, but I have two terrific sons.

So, the future looks reasonably good for Mark Read, so long as he lives long enough to see it. I have hepatitis C and that has slowed me down a lot; along with all the other things you accumulate in fifty-six years of pretty hard living.

I probably got hep C in the 1970s, because Pentridge inmates were made to share razor blades when we shaved. There would be two razor blades between all of us and they would only be changed once a week.

Eventually, I had to take a stand against this, which was when they started giving us individual disposable razor blades. It was too late for a lot of us, who have ended up with hep C.

I did say last year that I wouldn't have a liver transplant because I wouldn't want to deny someone such as a seven-year-old kid the chance to prolong their life. But if and when the times comes that there is a spare liver, well, we'll wait and see. I do want to see Charlie and Roy grow up, and share in as much of their lives as I can.

I have been off the grog for three and a half years now. I do miss it but it is better to have no grog and live a bit longer. My preferred drink these days is a cup of tea; or a raspberry lemonade, if I am down at the pub.

IT'S NINE years since the first day of the rest of my life that I started this book by telling you about. Where will I be in another nine years?

Hopefully, I will still be alive. That would be a great start. I've already outlived most of my enemies, except maybe Mick Gatto. And we're mates these days. I reckon Mick will die of a heart attack while he's on a golf course.

If I am still alive, I hope I will be living up in Queensland with Margaret. That's where we both want to go. We'd like a three-bedroom, double-storey house near the beach, with a heated swimming pool, split-system air-conditioning, a nice space for the car, and room for a nice pet. Margaret and I both like dogs. It is nice to have a house with a dog in it, as they fill the house up.

While I was writing this book, our wonderful old dog, Kyser, passed on. We were very saddened by his death. We had him cremated and his ashes brought home, and didn't go out and get another dog straightaway. It really is a hard business having dogs put down; it's part of being a dog owner, as dogs don't live as long as humans. Committing to another dog was not something we wanted to rush into. Margaret and I both like Staffordshire terriers, so I guess I'd like eventually to get an American Staffordshire terrier. They're an intelligent breed and people friendly.

I reckon that in nine years' time, I'll be considered an elder statesman of sorts. Soon, I'll be singing to Margaret to ask her if she'll still need me, and if she'll still feed me when I'm sixty-four.

I bloody well hope her answer is yes.

So, a few years down the track, if you're up in Queensland and you see this old bloke with lots of tattoos, but missing a couple of ears, out walking his American Staffordshire terrier, make sure you walk up and say, 'G'day, Mark.'

Or Chopper. I don't mind what you call me.

I'll be feeling pretty relaxed about most things, I'm sure.

I've got a sign out the front of my house in Collingwood that says, 'This house is guarded by a shotgun three days a week, you pick which three days.' I don't think I'll need to take it with me.

In *Chopper the Musical*, there's a line about it being easier for your enemies to get you when you're relaxed. But, if I make it to sixty-four, I don't reckon there'll be too many of my enemies left.

I will have outlived them all. Ha ha!

ACKNOWLEDGEMENTS

A book like this doesn't get written without a lot of help from a lot of people.

First and foremost, I want to thank my wife, Margaret, for steering me through the months of writing, and making cups of tea and buying the odd wonderful cream donut.

And for prodding me whenever I fell asleep.

I have to thank Margaret for a lot of other things too – for writing her own chapters, and also convincing my mother to make her small contribution. Margaret also organised the trip to Tasmania in April of this year, when we had a wonderful four days with Mum.

I am grateful for the support of my new manager, Andrew Parisi, and for his efforts in helping set up this project.

Thanks, too, to Tom Gilliatt and everyone else at my new publisher, Pan Macmillan.

I am very grateful to Margaret's brother, Ron Cassar, who had the hectic job of keeping my son Roy occupied as I was working away on the book. Ron is a terrific uncle to him.

I would also like to thank Warwick Hadfield.

And, while I am at it, thanks to everyone who some-where, somehow, along the way, helped ensure that Mark Brandon Chopper Read got to live to the ripe old age of fifty-six, planning many more years to come.

Who said he'd never make it?